About this Learning Guide

Shmoop Will Make You a Better Lover*
*of Literature, History, Poetry, Life...

Our lively learning guides are written by experts and educators who want to show your brain a good time. Shmoop writers come primarily from Ph.D. programs at top universities, including Stanford, Harvard, and UC Berkeley.

Want more Shmoop? We cover literature, poetry, bestsellers, music, US history, civics, biographies (and the list keeps growing). Drop by our website to see the latest.

www.shmoop.com

Table of Contents

Introduction

In a Nutshell

Nectar in a Sieve is <u>Kamala Markandaya</u>'s first published novel. This narrative focuses on the story of one woman living in poverty in rural India during a time of great change. Though the book meticulously avoids specifics about the time and place of the story, some context clues give us a sense that the work is an exploration of socioeconomic and political issues in the novelist's contemporary India. We see these often controversial issues addressed by the protagonist, Rukmani (who is also called Ruku).

India's political situation isn't explicitly discussed, but there is enough to glean that Markandaya is writing about the changing political and economic situation in her country. She published *Nectar in a Sieve* in 1954, seven years after India gained colonial independence from Britain.

Many traditions in India were eroded by British rule, and the developments brought upon by the industrial revolution lured many young Indians away from their traditional roles to participate in a new economy. Such is the case with the arrival of the tannery in Rukmani's village, and the decision of her sons to leave the land for work of a different nature.

Ruku's literacy also points to reforms in India launched during the colonial period. The British introduced an educational system that allowed many Indians to explore the importance of justice and freedom. Ruku's sons rely less on traditional religious notions of the good of suffering, and more on ideas about the importance of political freedom and economic security.

Starvation was a certainty that Markandaya knew firsthand. In 1943 starvation in Bengal of epidemic proportions claimed the lives of over three million people. Markandaya describes hunger in *Nectar in a Sieve* with reference to a starving people, who are sometimes willing to do anything in order to feed themselves. People's attitude towards the new spectrum of economic opportunities is tempered by the cruelty of the natural environment on which they rely.

Tension between Hindus and Muslims are subtly addressed in *Nectar in a Sieve*. This kind of tension between two very different religions and cultures was and continues to be a controversial issue. India's independence also coincided with the creation of Pakistan, a new state largely populated by Muslims who had left India. This departure of Muslims resulted in India being a largely Hindu nation. Rukmani's interactions with the Muslim woman in the novel reveal to our protagonist that many different kinds of lives can be contained in one country. Social roles for women were also changing in post-independence India, and what a woman valued, as well as how she herself should be valued within society, are raised as questions in the novel.

The book also investigates the teachings of <u>Gandhi</u>, leader of India's freedom movement. Markandaya discusses such issues as the importance of freedom and rights alongside the importance of spiritual purity and goodness. All of these religious, cultural, economic, social, and

political issues are deftly crafted into this personal narrative. Ultimately, *Nectar in a Sieve* provides infinite doors through which to explore these universal themes in the face of a changing society.

Summary

Book Summary

We meet our narrator Rukmani as an elderly woman, looking back over the events of her life. At the very onset Ruku (a nickname for Rukmani) launches into her life-story, describing what it means to be desperate and poverty stricken in rural 20th century India.

Rukmani begins her flashback reflecting on her marriage to Nathan. Ruku was the fourth daughter of a once-important village headman. As their wealth and status dwindled, it was hard to scrape together a dowry (money or possessions a woman would bring to her husband when married) for Ruku. As a result this fourth daughter was married to Nathan, a poor tenant farmer with no land, but a noble man nonetheless with heart of gold. Ruku settles into a simple farming life very happily, as Nathan is kind and loving with her. The main problem, though, is that she has had only one child, a daughter named Ira, after six years of marriage.

Ruku desperately wants sons, because giving birth to boys is a point of pride in Indian culture. So she pours her heart out to Kenny, a white doctor whom our protagonist first met when he was helping her dying mother. Ruku undergoes fertility treatment despite the fact that she never mentions it to her husband, Nathan. It must've been pretty potent medicine, as Ruku has five sons in the next few years. The family is happy enough, but with all these new mouths to feed, money is tight.

Big changes arrive with the construction of a tannery, where animal skins are cured. The noisy process disturbs Ruku, as she watches her home transformed from a quiet village to a dirty town. Other big changes come as Ira grows older and turns fourteen, the traditional age of marriage. A friendly member of the village, Old Granny, finds Ira a nice match through the common practice of arranged marriage. Ira's groom is the sole inheritor of some land, and many members of the village turn out for the joyful but modest celebration.

Ira leaves for her husband's home, and immediately thereafter, a terrible monsoon strikes. It seems as if the heavens are crying out in agony at the departure of the only daughter. The family faces near-starvation for the first time, but get to eat again when the rains end. Nathan and the sons harvest rice and hunt fish living in the wet fields.

However, it's not long before disaster strikes again. Ira's husband delivers Ira back to her parents' home because she has failed to conceive a child. The family's thin resources become stretched again, and Ruku's two eldest sons go to work in the tannery to make extra money. Their decision to seek work outside of the land dashes Nathan's hopes that his sons will take after him. The tannery jobs are good for a while though, and bring in some much-needed money. As a result the relative financial security the family experiences, they decide to celebrate

the Festival of Lights, Deepavali Deepavali. On that joyous night, Ruku conceives her last baby.

Buoyed by the improving situation, Ruku seeks help from Kenny for Ira's infertility (still keeping these treatments a secret from Nathan). One evening she is caught on a late night visit to Kenny by Kunthi, her old neighbor. In a scramble, Kunthi threatens to reveal what she knows about Ruku's illicit visits to Kenny, and implies not-so-subtly that Ruku is having an affair. During their brief conversation Ruku realizes that Kunthi has turned to prostitution.

Ruku then makes another visit, this time to Ira's former husband. Unfortunately, he has already married a new woman and won't take Ira back (in spite of the recent fertility treatments). Ruku begins to realize that Ira maybe never leave home.

She encounters more grief when her educated sons start a strike at the tannery, petitioning for better wages. Ira is moody, the boys (now out of work because of scabs at the tannery) have grown sullen and distant, and Ruku feels like she no longer knows her children. Eventually, Arjun and Thambi, Ruku's two eldest sons, answer a call for work at a tea plantation in Ceylon (now known as Sri Lanka). She and Nathan let them go hesitantly, believing that they'll never see the boys again. Ruku has "lost" another son too, as Kenny has found her third boy, Murugan, work as a servant in a distant city.

More ills befall the family. There's a drought that season, which means no harvest. They sell off all their goods (but save their seed), hoping to make up half the rent for the land. Rukmani has saved up a little food to get them through, but Kunthi blackmails Rukmani to give up half of what she's saved. Right after, she realizes the other half of food that remained is gone too. In an emotional exchange, Nathan reveals Kunthi extorted the rest of the rice from him. Kunthi threatened to reveal the fact that two of her sons were fathered by Nathan. Ruku and Nathan forgive each other, the air is clear between them, and yet they still face starvation.

In the meantime, Raja, Ruku's fourth son, is killed at the tannery. His body is brought home. Soon after, tannery men visit to explain the death. Apparently Raja was trying to steal a calfskin and was so weak from hunger, that he fell dead when they beat him in punishment. They insist the tannery has no responsibility.

Things only worsen for Ruku and her family as they continue face starvation. The youngest child, Kuti, is taking it particularly hard. He's weak and whimpering, but suddenly seems to start to get better.

One night, Ruku has a fight with a woman who is sneaking into their house late at night, thinking it's Kunthi. It turns out to be Ira, who has turned to prostitution to bring money in to feed Kuti. Ruku doesn't understand Ira's decision, but she can't stop her daughter, and besides, Kuti needs the food. In spite of the fact that the family does everything they can to feed the young boy, Kuti dies. In an ironic turn of events, the family has a rich harvest immediately after Kuti's death.

Selvam, Ruku's last remaining son, decides to leave the land and instead become Kenny's assistant at the hospital. (By the way, did we mention that Kenny is building a hospital with funding from India and abroad?). Ruku accepts this piece of news, and then turns her attention

to Ira, who is now pregnant with the child of one of her clients.

In another blow, the family's embarrassment is augmented when they learn that Ira's baby has a rare skin pigment disease known as albinism. Though the village is curious, Selvam chides everybody for being foolish: a baby is a baby and deserves love and attention. Eventually, everyone learns to accept the baby in spite of the fact that he looks different.

The family, as usual, is cobbling a life together, when the worst news of all comes. Sivaji, the man who collects dues for the landowner, arrives to announce to Nathan that the land he (Nathan) has rented for thirty years has been bought by the tannery. The family must leave their home in two weeks.

Nathan and Ruku are distraught and shocked. Nathan is too old to work on the land, and he can't imagine setting up a new place. The whole family must make new plans. Nathan and Ruku will have to move in with Murugan, their son in the city whom they haven't heard from in years. Ira and her baby, Sacrabani, will stay behind and live with Selvam.

Ruku and Nathan make the long journey to the unnamed city, only to discover that their son Murugan has deserted his wife and is no where to be found. Murugan's wife has turned the prostitution, so their first meeting with her is somewhat less than joyful. Simply put, there's no way she'll be able to keep them. The old couple is basically out on their own: all their goods and their money were stolen earlier on the journey, and they have nowhere to stay.

They end up taking refuge in a temple where the city's destitute are fed dinner and given shelter. All they can think of is returning home. Ruku decides to make a little money by setting up as a letter-writer and reader in the market. Business isn't great, but every little bit helps.

Things take a turn for the better when Puli, a street orphan whom Ruku and Nathan met on the way to find Murugan's house, shows up again in their life. Puli is fiercely independent, but he has leprosy, a serious illness that has taken his fingers. He unofficially adopts Nathan and Ruku, and he comes up with the plan of working at a stone quarry, gathering rocks for pay. With this job, Ruku, Nathan, and Puli establish something of a family routine, and begin saving up money to return to their village.

Just as they begin to have enough money, Nathan becomes ill. In spite of his illness, Nathan insists on working at the quarry. One day as Ruku is following behind him home, she finds he has collapsed into a ditch in convulsions. Helpful onlookers carry Nathan back to the temple, and Ruku holds him in her arms through the night, ministering to him as he dies.

Ruku and Puli return to the village, where Selvam, Ira, and Sacrabani greet them. Ira immediately warmly welcomes Puli, while Selvam and Ruku walk a little behind them, addressing the conspicuous absence of Nathan. Selvam assures his mother they will find some way to manage.

Chapter One

- Our heroine begins her narration in the present, though her story will be about the past. She begins by talking wistfully about her husband, who is no longer with her, except in her dreams.
- Her waking life, we learn, is peopled with loved ones: her daughter, a little boy named Puli (who has no fingers, and doesn't actually belong to her family, though she keeps and loves him), and her son Selvam, who works with a man called Kenny in a hospital.
- The narrator explains she is an old woman now. She begins to tell us her story.
- Her father was a "headman" in her village, a position that became less important when a figure called "the collector "began to change the dynamics of village politics.
- Our narrator was the youngest of four daughters, and as her father's importance dwindled, her own prospects for a suitable arrangement of marriage to a young man diminished too.
- Her parents could not afford a grand dowry (money given to the groom's family by the bride's family), and the best they can do was marry her to a poor tenant farmer.
- Though our narrator tells us her family lamented the match, she herself was happy with the arrangement. At the time of her marriage, she was twelve.
- The woman describes her simple union to her husband, Nathan. We learn that Nathan is gentle and caring. On the six-mile ride to her new home, she cries *and* gets sick. Nathan does his best to comfort her.
- She's happy enough with the idyllic country ride, until she arrives at her new "home," which is really a two-room mud hut complete with thatched roof beside a rice paddy field.
- Our narrator tries to hide her displeasure, saying she's worn out from the ride, but Nathan senses her unease and tries to comfort her. He promises a better future and presents her with handfuls of grain from a good rice harvest. On this, he says, they'll rest their future.
- Our narrator then describes her adjustment to domestic village life – she does laundry in the river and meets some of the local women, Kali, Janaki, and Kunthi. In their talk with our narrator, we finally learn her name is Rukmani.
- From the women's friendly gossip, Rukmani learns that Nathan was unbelievably excited about his marriage to Rukmani, and that he built their home with his own two hands, sometimes even neglecting his work in the field to provide the best home he could.
- Rukmani has a poignant moment of recognition as she learns what she means to Nathan. Nathan, in turn, demurs modestly when Rukmani confronts him about why he never told her that this house was his own handiwork.
- Rukmani-as-narrator then nostalgically glosses over those happy days, and she says she's glad to have had those good times, as she can look back on them and remember that once her life was blessed.
- Rukmani then fills us in on more details: while Nathan doesn't own the land he works, there is still a chance that he might one day have enough money to buy it. In the meantime, they eat well and are even able to store some rice from each harvest. Rukmani delights in trips to the market, meeting the local characters: a jovial old woman who sells guava and peanuts (named, fittingly, Old Granny), a shady moneylender, and Kunthi, her neighbor who is not particularly warm or friendly.
- Rukmani notes that people often say Kunthi married below. People might say the same of Rukmani, but even she admits she's not much of a looker. Also she didn't know much about how to work the land, so on all fronts, she wasn't much of a catch.

- Rukmani then describes the things she learned from the friendly neighborhood women: milking the goat, planting seed, churning butter, and mulling rice.
- Rukmani's first pumpkin plant is a particularly memorable victory: it yields generously, and when she brings a pumpkin in to Nathan, he's tremendously proud of her.
- Flush with success and a bit of pride at her growing achievement, Rukmani grows different kinds of plants, and the eating is good.

Chapter Two

- Our heroine helps Kunthi give birth to her child: Rukmani is the lone helper as the midwife is nowhere to be found.
- When Rukmani finally returns home to Nathan after a long day's birthing, Nathan is very cross: his wife is pregnant herself and shouldn't put herself or her baby in danger.
- Since she is pregnant, Rukmani now has time to do non-work activities. We learn that her father taught all of his children to read and write. Perhaps he educated his children for prestige, but it is more likely it is because he knew reading and writing in difficult times could be a gentle pleasure.
- Reactions to Rukmani's literacy vary: her mom is not behind all this fancy book-learning, especially for girls. Kali (the gossipy village lady) scorns Rukmani's writing as something she'll have to give up once she's busy with real women's work.
- Nathan's reaction is best though. Nathan watches Rukmani write, leaves to ruminate on it, and then returns, stroking her hair and praising her for her cleverness. Rukmani notes that his reaction demonstrates his maturity – though he is illiterate, he can be comfortable with his wife's strengths – different though they are from his.
- We get a garden update too: as the plants grow, Rukmani shares that she is utterly delighted with the garden, where each tiny seed protects the secret of life. After a startling (but harmless) encounter with a cobra in her garden, Rukmani's own tiny seed soon comes springing into the world. She gives birth to a baby girl, and she weeps over the misfortune.
- The couple names the little girl Irawaddy, after one of Asia's great rivers, the rationale being that water was the most precious thing in the world. Though Nathan, too, would have preferred a boy to be his heir and namesake, he grows to love Ira as soon as she learns to say "Apa," meaning father.
- As a child, Ira is a marvelous beauty, which is a bit puzzling for her ordinary-looking parents. She is energetic and good-natured, too, and entertains herself while her parents go about their domestic and rural duties.
- Ira is actually such a joy that Rukmani's mother often endures the long ride to come and see her. Rukmani notes that she unfortunately does not go to see her mother that often, because she's busy at home. Her mother, far from being angry, understands.

Chapter Three

- Ira is now approaching her sixth birthday, and she is still an only child. Rukmani quietly worries that she and Nathan will only have one child, and a girl at that.
- The village women gossip and pray, and Rukmani's mother even gives her a tiny stone sculpture for good luck. Unfortunately, nothing seems to work.
- Ruku's mother begins to die of the consumption. Kennington, affectionately dubbed Kenny, is a doctor who mysteriously appears. Kenny speaks their language and strives to makes himself useful.
- Kenny is the first white person Rukmani has ever seen, so she stares at him. Ruku's appreciates Kenny's efforts, but believes that he's powerless to actually do anything useful.
- Rukmani's mother passes away peacefully, and Rukmani goes to thank the doctor. Kenny somehow understands that Rukmani is having fertility issues."
- At first, Rukmani hesitates to tell Kenny anything. In the first place, he's a strange man she doesn't know. More importantly, however, she hasn't told *anyone* about what's going on. Finally, though, Rukmani's grief pours out as she explains she has only one child, and a daughter at that.
- After her confession, Rukmani shrinks away from being so open, as she realizes she'd never seen a doctor of his kind before. Kenny senses her fear and calls her foolish. Rukmani slinks away, but eventually comes back to seek treatment.
- Soon after, Rukmani has her first child in seven years and it's a boy. Even though he is quite advanced in age, Rukmani's father journeys six miles in a bullock cart just to see his grandson. Nathan is overjoyed and organizes a big feast so that the whole village can meet the new son.
- There's cooking and eating and music, and even Kunthi (who has grown distant with time) came to celebrate the new child. Rukmani is happy during the feast, but she notes the absence of the person she most wished to see: Kenny. It was the doctor, after all, who made the baby possible.
- Rukmani then reveals that she hasn't been honest with Nathan about the medical help she got from Kenny. Initially, she didn't know what Nathan's reaction would be. She reasoned that she would tell her husband about her visits to the foreigner only if she succeeded in having a baby.
- Of course, now that Rukmani has had the baby, were she to tell Nathan about he help she had, Nathan would wonder why she had deceived him. Basically, to not have to deal with admitting a lie, Rukmani decides to keep lying. She then asserts that it isn't *lying* so much as "preserving silence."
- Rukmani proceeds to have five sons in a row. Thambi, Murugan, Raja, and Selvam follow Arjun. Ira, meanwhile, is growing up. Rukmani confides that Ira only began to wear clothes when she turned five. Since that time, Ira has been a tremendous help in raising the boys, especially as she is so good with children.
- With six kids to feed, things really begin to change around Ruku's house. Rukmani begins to sell the best vegetables she grows, keeping only the bruised and spoiled ones to feed her family. Old Granny (remember the old lady who sells at market?) is Rukmani's chief buyer, and she's always full of praise for Rukmani's healthy vegetables.
- Rukmani is happy to do business with Old Granny too, until the day when she is stopped

by Biswas, the crude moneylender. For her vegetables, he offers her nearly twice what Old Granny pays. Though Rukmani is reluctant to change her allegiance, money talks. Rukmani begins to sell nearly everything to Biswas, leaving only a little for the old woman out of kindness. Old Granny never complains, though Rukmani feels compelled to explain that things are getting harder at home.

- Recently, they've been cutting down on nicer things, like milk (except for the baby) and butter (except on special occasions). Still, unlike many other families, they've never gone hungry. They grow their own plantains and coconuts, and they always manage to put aside a little rice from the harvests. There's even fish to be had from the rice paddy fields. With a little resourcefulness, they are getting by, and Rukmani seems especially grateful that every month, she can even save a rupee or two for Ira's dowry.

Chapter Four

- Construction begins on a tannery (where animal hides are cured for other uses) in Rukmani's village. The building of the tannery is quite a spectacle. Lots of men from the outside world come in with carts and bricks. The colonial structure is in place here, too: there is an Indian boss oversees the builders; a white man oversees the entire operation.
- The tannery changes how people work in the village: the building workmen are paid well, and the village people are occupied in supplying their mounting needs, from rope and bricks to fruit and sweetmeats. The workmen bring in their families and live in little huts with them, mostly isolated from villagers.
- In two months, the tannery is completed, and the workmen suddenly disappear. Everything is quiet in the village for a while, which gives people time to reflect on the influence of the workmen. While Rukmani resented the noise brought with them, she, like many others, benefited economically from being able to sell to the workers.
- Rukmani regrets that the tannery has come to her village. Nathan assures her that they will be back, and there's nothing that can be done about it. Sure enough, Nathan is right: new men replace the men who left. They bring their wives and families, but they also bring pollution, the stink of liquor brewing, their noisy habits, and all-around calamity.
- The tannery also results in new parental restrictions for Ira. Up until this time, Ira had been allowed to roam freely, but neighbors notice that suddenly the men are paying attention to the young girl. She is beautiful, if only thirteen. Rukmani and Nathan suddenly curtail her freedom to protect her from the workmen, and to protect the family from gossip. Though Ira resents the new limitations, she is obedient.

Chapter Five

- Rukmani and Nathan live as tenants on the land that belongs to a Zemindar, (landowner). Still, the couple has never actually met the Zemindar, because a messenger named Sivaji acts on his behalf. Sivaji is kind and judicious and treats the tenants fairly. He doesn't demand bribes or steal from the fields.

- Rukmani is collecting dung from the fields one day when she spots Kenny, whom she hasn't seen in a long time. She and Kenny have a characteristic exchange – sharp but still light. Kenny notes that the dung belongs to the land, and is good for it, but Rukmani has a quiet rejoinder. The dung is used as a fuel and seal for the houses, and protects them from damp, heat, and pests. While Kenny criticizes the negative environmental impact, he has no response when Rukmani's asks what else the people might use.
- Kenny then visits Rukmani's modest home. He's gracious, especially with Nathan, and compliments him for having a household rich in good women and many sons. Rukmani hears this and panics, because she *still* hasn't told Nathan about the fertility treatments. To date, Rukmani has only spoken of Kenny as a great help to her parents.
- Kenny quickly becomes a friend of the house. While he is quiet about his own personal life, he adapts easily to of the love of Rukmani's children for him, and he returns it in his own quiet way. He would even bring gifts, such as coconut. Kenny also learns that things are getting harder for Ruku's family. They've had to sell the goat and cannot otherwise afford to buy milk. As a result, Ruku is still breast-feeding her three-year-old son. Kenny does not pity them openly, but he then brings milk for the baby when he can.
- For all this new friendship, Kenny remains mysterious. As far as Rukmani knows, he works for the tannery on occasion and spends his long days tending to the sick, only to go return to his empty house. Kenny also has a penchant for disappearing without explanation. No one knows where he goes, but it's clear that he returns in a worse mood every time.

Chapter Six

- Irawaddy is fourteen, two years older than Rukmani was when she married. Rukmani can no longer put off the girl's wedding, and begins to look for a suitable matchmaker. She chooses Old Granny, who is old and experienced in such matters. Though Rukmani has not done business with Old Granny for years, the old woman bears her no grudge and is happy to help.
- Because Rukmani's family is not well-off, Ruku worries they'll not be able to find a suitable match for Ira. They can only afford a dowry of 100 rupees. Their daughter is beautiful, though, and this is worth a lot. Old Granny is able to find a handsome young man who is sole heir to his father's generous portion of land.
- Ira is agrees to the marriage, but she is clearly wistful. Though Ruku is happy that she's found a good match, she can't help but reflect on her own marriage as a young girl. Ruku knows that Ira will have to bear the pain of separation, and the jolt of a new place. Still, Ruku promises to visit her daughter two or three times a year.
- The wedding is a joyous celebration of food and music, though Nathan insists on having nothing they can't afford easily, as he hates the idea of debts. Rukmani has put aside a fair share of delicacies she's been saving up month by month for the occasion. Still, there's a reminder of hard times when she sees her son Arjun with a little bundle. He's not eating heartily at the feast itself, but has hoarded a little bit for later.
- Ira looks younger than her years in her makeup and her mother's red wedding sari. She looks frightened by the whole affair, especially when the time comes for her to depart with her new husband. A happy crowd lifts her and her husband into the air, decking them with

flower garlands and good wishes.

- After Ira leaves, the crowd melts and the clamor dies down. Ruku returns to her home. There is work to be done tomorrow, mending and cleaning, but as Ruku returns to her husband's side for the night, she lays awake, thinking. It is the first night her daughter has not slept under their roof.

Chapter Seven

- With all the preparation for Ira's marriage, Nathan did little to weatherproof their house and prepare for the coming monsoon season. Rukmani notes that nature is like a wild animal that strikes when you're unprepared. Ironically, the rains strike early and more fiercely than ever.
- The rain is incessant, and the hut itself (made of mud walls) would have been washed away had Nathan not built it on high ground. The house is filled with vessels to catch the rainwater, but soon leaks outnumber pots in the house. The family tries to make do with a little firewood left over from Ira's wedding, but their problems do not end.
- As the rain worsens, the paddy fields drown and the crops become destroyed. Nathan, characteristically lean of words, simply declares that there will be little eating this year. There was already a shortage of food, and the prospect of having even less breaks the boys, who sit in a huddle on the wet floor and weep.
- The storm gives way to lightning on the eighth night. The paddy fields are already ruined, and now the coconut tree, which fed the family often, is struck by lightning. Yet another food source is lost.
- After the fiery night, the world seems to have calmed, and Rukmani and Nathan come out to survey the damage. The garden, the cornfield, and the rice paddy are now gone.
- Many neighbors lost even more: six men died and Kali's hut is completely destroyed. Kali even comes to Ruku's house to ask for some coconut palms so that she might thatch her house again. Rukmani cannot help, as what little is left of the burnt coconut tree must be used for her own home.
- Nathan and Rukmani prepare to go to the market to get rice and palm leaves from the village.
- Nathan inspects their bundle of money buried in the granary, and Rukmani remembers how it was once heavy at the time of their wedding. Now it is a limp and sad bundle, amounting to only twelve rupees. They plan to use no more than two rupees for the repairs.
- The couple set off to market. On the way they survey the debris of the storm. Shacks and huts, trees, sticks, and stones lie in a ruckus on the streets, but the tannery building stands strong.
- As Nathan and Rukmani encounter more signs of the disaster that has struck the village, they decide to return home, as it's likely no one will yet have anything to sell.
- At home, they meet their hopeful children empty-handed, and again the children weep from despair and hunger. With nothing to tell the little ones, Rukmani simply lays awake and listens to the drums of calamity beating doom over the whole land.
- The couple set out again the next day, and find Hanuman the rice merchant. They try to

negotiate a fair price for the rice. Food is in short supply, though, and everyone is seeking it: their two precious rupees must be spent on a mere two pounds of rice. Even this is a bargain, Hanuman contends, as the workmen from the tannery would pay more.

- On the way home, Nathan and Rukmani run into Kenny, who looks a straight mess. Despondent but straight-shooting, he concludes that this family is starving and hears Rukmani reply that they have a little rice, enough to tide them over for now. Kenny flares up at this, and then begins to curse them for their meekness. He contends that things won't get better quickly, and that they should be crying out for the help they so badly need.
- Kenny seems in utter despair about the country of India and the people who live here. Rukmani and Nathan interpret Kenny's outburst as pure madness. They leave him to his raving.
- Things start to look better at home though: there is ample fish in the drowned paddy and some of the grain has survived. Still, there is not much available food.
- The family stays up late cleaning the fish and separating the rice grains from the husk. When they eat, it is with a pleasant surprising feeling that they have enough food for now. Rukmani dreams of what their food stores, and the new vegetables she'll grow. She falls into a deep peaceful sleep.

Chapter Eight

- Things are less than ideal with the village neighbors. Kunthi's two eldest sons have begun working at the tannery, and the woman insists that this business is a great boon.
- Of course, Rukmani is less happy about the tannery. This shouldn't surprise us though, because Kunthi and Rukmani are opposites in just about every way. Rukmani is proud to be a woman of the earth, while Kunthi claims she can never be such a simple and natural creature.
- The other great scandal is that the beautiful Kunthi has been walking the town and attracting the attention of men. Her husband does nothing to rein her in, and she's quickly walking down the road to harlotry.
- Janaki has troubles of a different sort. Janaki's husband's shop has not been doing well, because it can't withstand the competition from the big shopkeepers funded by the tannery.
- Rukmani recounts with some wistfulness the day that Janaki's family suddenly came to say goodbye, with their meager belongings on their back. Who knows what new life they'll find. Rukmani, however, has no time to consider such things, and soon enough Janaki and her family are forgotten.
- We get some more detail about the tannery. Besides white men, the tannery has brought in Muslims, who live in a separate compound. The Muslims' compound is markedly wealthier than the one inhabited by the other villagers.
- Rukmani notes that the Muslim men are hard workers, but the women are more mysterious creatures. These women employ servants to do their errands outside of the house, and when they travel they do so in the head-to-toe veil of the bourka.
- Rukmani feels sorry for these women, who are kept shuttered in their houses away from

the sunlight and green fields that she so loves. Still, Kali points out, they live lavishly, and without need. Kali's husband notes that it's a trade-off,.

- Rukmani meets a Muslim woman when she (Rukmani) is asked to make a house visit to sell vegetables. In order to see what she is buying, the woman removes her veil.
- Unlike the other women of the village, this woman is pale and dainty. On the Muslim woman's hands are rings that could easily feed Ruku's family for years.
- Still, Rukmani is disturbed by the quiet sadness that pervades the shuttered house, and never goes there again.

Chapter Nine

- Rukmani is pounding chilies one morning when she spots Ira and her son-in-law approaching. She's ready to greet them joyfully, but soon realizes that they are not on a happy errand.
- Ira's husband is courteous but cool. He explains that it has been five years, and Ira has not given him a child, let alone a son. As she is unable to fulfill her chief wifely duty, she is no wife. Her husband leaves her behind.
- Nathan takes this rejection of his daughter in stride, saying her husband cannot be blamed because he's already been patient. Rukmani remembers the grief of her barren period and sees her daughter's pain as her own. She tries in vain to comfort her. Her mind wanders to Kenny, and wonders if he can help.
- Two more blows fall on Rukmani's family. Much to Ruku's dismay, her two eldest sons, Arjun and Thambi, decide to work at the tannery. Arjun had taken to the learning his mother had given them, and even eventually surpassed his mother in reading and writing. When he announces his decision to work in the tannery, he justifies it as a way to bring food to their family.
- Arjun notes that there is never enough to eat, especially since Ira has returned home. Rukmani is crestfallen at his criticism, but knows there is nothing she can do to stop him. A second injury comes from Arjun's insistence that he can get a tannery job with help from Kunthi's son. Rukmani has grown distant from Kunthi, and she (Rukmani) doesn't want to be indebted to her neighbor.
- Rukmani quickly volunteers to have Kenny help. Arjun suggests that the closeness Rukmani feels for Kenny is more than friendship, implying that his mother has been unfaithful with Kenny.
- Thambi, Rukmani's second son, has always been very close to Arjun, so his decision to follow Arjun to work at the tannery is no surprise.
- Thambi launches a further insult at Nathan. Nathan says he's always wanted sons because they could work beside him on the land, but Thambi cruelly points out that the land is the Zemindar's, so anyone working on it only helps to fill the Zemindar's pockets.
- Nathan is crushed: Thambi's words confirm the sad suspicion that neither he nor his sons will ever own the land on which they've worked for so long.
- Despite the terrible circumstances under which the two boys gain their employment, the family still benefits from the money they earn. Once again the family can eat properly, and Rukmani can even keep a little food on the side. She is able to keep some chilies, which

offset the plainness of their rice diet. Also, she can finally fix the thatch of the roof.

- She's even able to buy new clothes, including garments for the children, a sari for herself, and a dhoti for Nathan, who badly needed one. She notes that she and Nathan still had the nice clothes they wore at Ira's wedding, but they are preserving those for the happy days of their sons' weddings.
- In spite of everything, Rukmani looks hopefully to the future.

Chapter Ten

- It is time for Deepavali, the Festival of Lights, and the entire village is in a celebratory mood.
- Flush with the new wealth of her sons' work in the tannery, Rukmani indulges in the extravagance of fireworks. Her qualms about spending are calmed by the children's joy.
- They celebrate at home, eating well and playing with sparklers and fireworks. Soon their celebration moves to the town.
- Selvam, Ruku's youngest, is the most serious and stubborn of the boys. Frightened by the noise of the celebration, he stays behind at the house with Ira. (Ira has been trying to stay away from the town's gossip, and seems happy to have the distraction and excuse of caring for her little brother.)
- Rukmani describes the joy of the town's bonfire. It seems that people are putting their differences behind them: the workers from the tannery are celebrating with the villagers. The women are covered in flowers and bangles, with silver rings on their toes, and everyone generally looks joyous.
- Rukmani is captivated by the fiery crackle of the bonfire, and she loses herself in the crowd.
- When she finally finds Nathan, he is prancing about joyously, carrying his sons on his shoulders and hips.
- Ruku teases him that he's mad with drink. Nathan insists that he hasn't had a drop of alcohol, and hoists her joyously in the air, much to her embarrassed amusement. Nathan embraces the celebratory spirit and rejoices over his simple life, obedient children, and amazing wife.
- That night, once they return to the calm of home, Nathan's joy spills out into bed, and the two conceive their last child.

Chapter Eleven

- Nathan leaves the village to attend a male relative's funeral, and Rukmani finally gets the chance to seek fertility treatment for Ira. (Incidentally, we learn she has still not told her husband about Kenny's help.) Rukmani waits all day to see Kenny, and when she finally catches up with him, he is exasperated by the continued helplessness of the people around him.
- Still, he and Rukmani have their usual exchange, warm, but with an edge. Kenny says he

will try and help Ira, but makes no promises. As Ruku is leaving Kenny, she hears someone from the shadows whisper her name.

- To her surprise, she finds Kunthi, who taunts Rukmani cruelly about her whereabouts. She suggests that Rukmani is a passionate woman and implies that she has been unfaithful to Nathan. When Kunthi hints that she might confess all to Nathan, Ruku loses control of herself, and claws at her neighbor.
- In the scramble, Kunthi's sari slips from her body, and Rukmani is surprised to find she wears the marks of a prostitute: a low tied sari, and sandalwood paste smeared on her hips and below her breasts.
- Ruku is shocked, but she warns Kunthi to keep quiet about her night visit to Kenny, threatening that she can make things even worse for Kunthi. Kunthi slyly replies that she now has a powerful secret that could ruin Ruku and her husband. Kunthi then slinks back into the night.
- Ruku, back in the happy fold of a home, goes to Ira's husband to see if he'll take her back now that the infertility problem has been treated. Sadly, he grew tired of waiting and decided to remarry. Meanwhile, Ira has been in terrible spirits all this time; there is no trace of the happy girl she once was. The possibility that her husband might take her back only temporarily lightened her mood.
- We learn that Ruku is pregnant again. Ira only grows more foreign to her mother as Ruku blossoms in pregnancy. This ironic situation serves as a constant reminder of the one thing Ira cannot have. Ruku finally delivers the baby, and as he is tiny, he gets nicknamed "Kuti." The birth of Kuti brings out Ira's maternal instincts--she treats him as if he were her own.
- Ruku is happy for Ira's maternal transformation, but she is still troubled about Ira's future. They have no dowry for the girl, and it now common knowledge that she has lost her virginity and cannot conceive.
- Old Granny is upset about Ira's situation and tries to the distraught mother. She notes that she herself is an older woman living alone, and that she is doing fine. Ruku is not pleased at the prospect of Ira ending up the same way. Still, Old Granny insists she is fine. Ruku slowly stops grieving about Ira's future, though it occasionally torments her in her sleep.

Chapter Twelve

- Things seem to be going well at home. The family is able to live: Rukmani's sons dutifully bring her home their rupee per day, and Nathan continues to work the land. Ruku is able to put food aside for her family. She does, however, finally resign herself to the fact that she cannot save up for another dowry for Ira.
- Things take a turn for the worse when Ruku and Nathan visit Arjun and Thambi at the tannery. The parents learn that the workers (including the boys) are creating strife.
- Arjun and Thambi explain that they're being punished for agitating for better wages. The boys add that they are only doing what's right: they're thinking of their own livelihoods and the desire to start their own families.
- The workers' strife escalates, and eventually the boys join the other workers on strike. Ruku believes the boys have become spokesmen for the strike movement because they know how to read and write. Arjun and Thambi are out of work for a week before the

tannery calls a meeting for scabs to replace the striking workers.

- Ruku rails that it is futile to continue to fight, but the boys are prideful, and they say people will never learn if they cave in.
- Kali's sons have also been caught up in the strike, and she comes to complain. Nathan silences the squabble: the boys have made their own choices and that's that.
- Arjun and Thambi begin to come and go as they please, visiting the town at all hours. Their parents have lost control of them. One day, Selvam announces that new drums are being beaten in the town, and they are calling for workers. The boys go to investigate.
- When Arjun and Thambi return home, they speak with their parents, and confirm that the drums indeed beckoned workers. Nathan warily replies that he heard they were looking for workers in the far-off land of Ceylon.
- The boys are unperturbed – Ceylon or not, the wages are good, and the company will pay for the travel.
- Rukmani pleads that money isn't everything, but the boys counter that money is enough, especially since they have no land now. They are young, and work abroad calls. It does not suit young men to be idle.
- Arjun and Thambi assure their mother they will be back, but Rukmani fears they only make empty promises. She knows that if they leave, she will never see her two sons again. By the next morning, they are gone.
- We learn that Rukmani's third son, Murugan, has also left. He's gone to a city two days away to be a servant, and Kenny has helped him to get there with a recommendation.
- Nathan does his best to comfort Rukmani, who is near despair. He sits her down in the sunlight on the earth, and has her look around at the beauty of the land that keeps them. She notes that the tannery has driven away much of the wildlife.
- Still, Nathan shows her the grain growing in the rice stems, and once again encourages her to trust in the land, which promises a good harvest. Together, the two make hopeful plans to eat well this season and even to make enough to visit their sons.
- Kenny later meets Rukmani and brings good news that Murugan's employer is happy with him. In the closeness of the moment, Ruku inquires if Kenny does not have his own family he should be tending to. She momentarily seizes in a panic about being so forward, but Kenny responds. He wonders why it's taken her so long to ask.
- Kenny reveals that he has a wife and children back home. They wish he were not abroad, but has resisted their attempt to constrain him. He comes and goes as he pleases and is free to pursue his interests abroad. Still, he says he can only handle all the traveling in small doses.
- Kenny catches himself too, and saying he has revealed too much, and makes Ruku promise to never reveal the very personal information he has told her. He slinks away, and she only wonders after the mysterious, lonely figure.

Chapter Thirteen

- The family hits yet another crisis, as the rains fail and the crops dry out. The time for harvesting arrives, but there is nothing to show for it. Sivaji, the man who collects dues for the Zemindar, arrives promptly to ask for Nathan's rent. Of course, there is nothing to give

him.

- Hearing that Nathan has nothing to offer, Sivaji threatens that the land will be rented to another tenant who can pay.
- Nathan and Rukmani plead and argue, and finally Sivaji relents deciding that they can pay half now and the other half later.
- As Sivaji leaves, Nathan has a rare moment of angry despair: he curses that men like Sivaji are hired to protect the overlord from seeing the fact that people must starve in order for him to be fat. Rukmani gently reminds Nathan that Sivaji is only doing his job.
- With this small hope of making half the rent to keep their land, Nathan and Rukmani count up all of the things they have to sell: pots, vessels, the eldest boys' shirts left behind, the bullocks that plowed the land, the new clothes bought for Deepavali, the last of their reserves of food, and even their wedding clothes, which they were saving for the boys' weddings.
- Basically, everything they had, except the land, is to be sold. The land, they hope, will eventually provide enough for them to recover.
- Rukmani bundles up all the goods and takes her bundle to Biswas, the cruel moneylender, to see what she can get. He delights in how far she's fallen, and he has little sympathy for her since everyone is in a similar condition of desperation.
- Rukmani is not to be out-smarted though, and when he undervalues her goods at 30 rupees, she demands 75, saying she knows a Muslim woman that will pay that much for them (which she doesn't). Ruku nearly walks out after she's made the bluff, but Biswas takes the bait and begrudgingly pays what she asks.
- When Rukmani sums up what she and Nathan have sold they count out 125 rupees, less of half of what is owed. Rukmani and Nathan then have a rare fight: Nathan would sell the seed they have left for a few rupees, while Rukmani says that would mean they would have nothing to harvest. It would be sacrificing the future for an uncertain present. Nathan finally comes down on Rukmani's side, and in the morning they face Sivaji with less than half of their promised sum.
- Again, there's a bit of a tiff with Sivaji. The collector eventually agrees that next time Nathan will pay what's owed and then some. As he is leaving, Sivaji has a moment of pause, and apologizes for his harshness. He explains gently that he only does what he must to feed his own family. He wishes them the best, and Rukmani, humbled by his humility, returns his warm wishes in hard times.
- The rains finally come, but everything in the fields has already died. It is too late.

Chapter Fourteen

- With the rains back, the family plants the little seed they have, and waits. There is nothing left to sell, nothing has grown to eat immediately, and Rukmani is forced to pull out the little reserve they have left.
- In the granary, she has buried about ten pounds of rice. Measuring it out day by day, she worriedly realizes they have enough food to eat for only 24 days. She hopes God will provide after that.
- Rukmani and Nathan are plagued with worry about what will come. Rukmani thinks of

going to Kenny for help, but he has disappeared again. They're on their own.

- One day Kunthi shows up and demands food from Rukmani. Ruku's neighbor is utterly delusional: her husband has left her, and it's clear she's delved deeper into prostitution. Kunthi declares she will be well once she is restored by the food that Rukmani must give her.
- Ruku explains that Kunthi's sons should take care of her, as Ruku has her own family to worry about.
- Kunthi cryptically says "My sons are not mine alone," and then begins to make bold threats against Ruku. Kunthi implies that Rukmani has had an affair with Kenny. Our heroine quickly thinks her honesty will defend her.
- Rukmani then remembers, though, her son's strange suggestion that white men have power over women and Ira's strange looks whenever Ruku was so eager to visit Kenny. Ruku also recognizes that she has deceived Nathan already about her infidelity treatment. Once Nathan learns of one lie, he can rightfully imagine many more.
- She's overcome with doubt and shame, and as she weeps, Kunthi hangs over her.
- Rukmani gives up seven days of rations to Kunthi and is made miserable by the thought that not much food remains. Haunted by the thought, she goes to the grain's hiding place to count the remaining rice. Imagine her surprise when she finds just one day's worth of rice!
- Rukmani is distraught, and immediately realizes that while Kunthi knew of the grain in the granary, no one but her family knew of this other secret hiding spot. Basically, if anyone took the rice, it must've been someone in the family. She crouches over the empty spot until dawn, when she goes in to her house accuse her own children.
- She takes the littlest one, Kuti, outside, and returns to begin screaming at the other three, Ira, Raja and Selvam. Nathan comes in from the fields, drawn in by Kuti's crying outside and the shouting within the house. Rukmani is cruel with madness, and Nathan intervenes.
- To Rukmani's shock, Nathan breaks down. He admits that he is the one who took the rice, and sobs that it was not for himself. He confesses that he had no choice to give it to someone else. Immediately, Rukmani goes to him to comfort him, but he pours out his heart, which is heavy with guilt.
- Nathan admits that he's the father of Kunthi's two sons. He gave all the rice to Kunthi, who blackmailed him into giving it away.
- Rukmani goes through a series of feelings, "disbelief, disillusionment, anger, reproach, pain." She calms herself by remembering that Kunthi is capable of evil. She then takes this as an opportunity to come clean about her own lies. Rukmani tells Nathan the truth about Kenny's help with her infertility, and of Kunthi's extortion.
- With the truth out, the air is now clear. Rukmani notes that Kunthi has been robbed of her power over them. More importantly, with the rice gone, there can be no more obsession and worrying of how to stretch it out over days. There's a freedom in this certainty.
- The family turns to desperate measures to eat – roaming the countryside for dropped fruits, catching crabs and even going through the gutters for food. Rukmani notes they were not alone in this desperation; hunger has turned neighbors and friends into competitors.
- Rukmani describes the onset of starvation in detail: hunger is a numbing that makes it impossible to think of anything but food. It also becomes impossible to eat since food becomes so unfamiliar.
- Rukmani watches the people around her literally become skin and bones, and imagines she must look the same. The entire family, the village, everyone it seems, is suffering, but

Kuti, the tiny baby, takes it hardest of all. He weakens to frailty, no longer asking for food, but simply weeping.

- Ira offers her paltry breast in solace – only that can silence the starving child.

Chapter Fifteen

- One day, Raja doesn't come home as usual. Eventually he's brought home dead. The two men who carried Raja home mutter an unsatisfying explanation about something having to do with money, and the fact that Raja fell as soon as they laid hands on him, as he was weak from hunger. Rukmani is too shocked by this point to hear their explanation, and Ira has begun to cry.
- Ruku at first chastises Ira, saying she should save her strength for more than tears. Soon, though, Ira's grief pools and flows in Rukmani.
- She observes Raja's body with an incredible degree of detachment. She explains though, that what she sees before her is only the body. She will worry only about caring for his body: tying up the jaw before rigor mortis sets in, and closing his dead eyes.
- Rukmani is matter-of-fact about the washing and bandaging of Raja, because the thing that matters is the spirit. The spirit of her son is gone, and it is for his spirit that the mother grieves.
- Rukmani describes the cremation of Raja. (Note the sudden present tense of her narrative.) Nathan prepares the funeral bier to carry the body, and the funeral drums summon neighbors and friends to the service. At sunrise, the men leave with the body to burn it, and the women stay behind. With the last beat of the funeral drum, the women know the body is all ashes. Raja is gone.
- Less than three days later, two men from the tannery come to see Rukmani and Nathan. They excuse that the tannery's no role in Raja's death. One man says the watchmen were only doing their duty to protect their property. Raja had stolen a calfskin, and only the necessary amount of violence was used against him.
- Rukmani notes her son would've had no use for a calfskin, but she does concede that it might have brought some money. She admits they themselves have no wealth.
- The real truth of the men's visit comes out finally as they batter Rukmani with reason: her sons were known troublemakers. Raja shouldn't have stolen anything, but he was caught and had to pay the consequences.
- Ultimately, the tannery is worried that Rukmani will bring some legal claim against them, perhaps seeking compensation. They came to make it perfectly clear that Raja's death was his own fault, and that they can be blamed for nothing.
- Rukmani is confused, as there is no compensation possible for death. The more timid of the two watchmen speaks up finally. He says very gently that Raja wasn't brutally treated; he was just tapped with a bamboo stick, and he fell, likely from hunger and weakness combined. He tries with quiet desperation to show sympathy and sorrow for Rukmani.
- The other man, though, is hell-bent on emphasizing that Raja's death was not the tannery's fault, as if he fears any sorrow on their part is some admission of guilt.
- The meaner man goes so far as to suggest that it'll be a little easier for Ruku, with one less mouth to feed. The thinner, meeker man makes a sudden and surprising act of raising

his hand to check his more aggressive companion.

- Things simmer once Rukmani, still in shock, agrees with the aggressive man that the tannery is not to blame.
- As the men ready to leave, it is Rukmani who must do the comforting. The smaller man is clearly uneasy about the sleazy work they've just done. Ruku assures him that it does not matter, but the man quietly replies that he is terribly sorry for her. He leaves, visibly clouded by shame and misery.

Chapter Sixteen

- As usual, life is difficult. Rukmani in particular worries how they'll be able to harvest this season's rice, as they're significantly weakened by starvation. The real concern, though, is that the paddy won't be ready for harvest for another three weeks.
- They've all endured thus far, but they worry that Kuti, who is not yet five, won't make it. He goes hungry, like the others, but he also can't sleep because of a horrible rash that covers his body and makes him claw at his skin, leaving sores and blisters. Ruku is concerned that he might die at any time.
- Suddenly, Kuti seems to be getting better. He stops whimpering and even sleeps. Rukmani is certain that the gods have answered their prayers for Kuti, and she goes to sleep peacefully. Waking before daylight, she hears footsteps approach the hut. All she can think is that the steps belong to Kunthi, who must have come back to take what little is left to steal.
- In a panicked fit, she quickly gets out of the hut, and hurls herself against the woman she sees approaching. Rukmani loses control of her senses, and throws her anger and hatred into beating the living daylights out of the intruder. She's shaken from that stupor as her pummeled victim cries, "Mother! *Mother!*" Nathan has rushed out to pull Rukmani from their daughter, Ira.
- Ira is badly beaten, and Nathan is furious at Rukmani for not recognizing their own daughter. Rukmani can only mutter in her defense that she thought it was Kunthi.
- The biggest surprise of the evening is that many of Ira's wounds and gashes came from the breaking of the glass she was wearing. Where she managed to get glass bangles, and why she's walking around with them at night only has one possible explanation: Ira has turned to prostitution.
- As Rukmani takes Ira's sari to the river to wash off the blood from the squabble, she sees a shining rupee drop from the folds of the garment into the water. As Ira rests, recovering from the wounds, and Kuti whimpers, ailing from hunger, Rukmani can no longer deny that her daughter has been dancing in the street for money.
- Rukmani wrestles over her concern for Ira, never speaking of it explicitly, but quite obviously pained. Ira has made up her mind to sell her body, however, and will not be deterred.
- Nathan is harsh with his daughter. He runs into Ira as he comes home from the fields at sunset, and the girl is dressed and ready for the night shift. He calls her out as a common strumpet, and a harlot, but she is unmoved. So long as there is hunger, Ira will find work, even if it's of a distasteful sort.

- Ira's parents have done their best to forbid her work, and she has decided to be disobedient. Rukmani resigns herself to the fact that there is nothing else to be done. With Ira's money, they can afford to eat again. Still, Nathan will not touch any of the food bought from the girl's work.
- The baby Kuti, though, is less discerning about where food comes from. He seems to get better in the first few days of Ira's patronage, but he begins to weaken again. One evening, he cries out to his mother weakly that he has lost his sight. Ruku is frightened but tries to calm him.
- Rukmani goes to Kuti when she hears him turn over. She notices that he's looking towards Ira with unseeing eyes. Rukmani holds him and sings to him, seeming to forget in those painful moments that it's clear the life has left his body. In his death, the marks of suffering have gone from his face. Rukmani notes painfully that she could not have wished for him to come back to the life of suffering that he has left.

Chapter Seventeen

- Kuti is gone, and in a cruel twist of fate, the harvest is splendid that season. Their bounty is unexpected: it's the second time the field has been planted that year, and the family anticipated meager returns because the land had had no time to rest.
- The family spends days preparing the rice. One episode leaves them in tears of laughter: they're standing amidst all the food that will feed them, with enough left over to sell, and observe each other, emaciated and sallow. Their appearance, and the promise that this starvation is in the past, is enough to break them into cathartic fits of laughter.
- Ruku and Nathan happily plan for the future, thinking of the crops they'll sell and vegetables they'll grow. Rukmani notes that nothing compares to standing before a good, gathered harvest, especially after so much strife. Far from resenting everything that befell them before the harvest came, the family is full of prayers of gratitude.

Chapter Eighteen

- Rukmani is coming back from the market one day when Biswas (remember the mean moneylender?) stops her. Rukmani has not done business with Biswas in a long time, as other shopkeepers pay better prices, and she doesn't have to endure the sly scorn Biswas tends to treat her with.
- Biswas delivers the news that Kenny has returned. He tries his best to insinuate that Ruku had an affair with Kenny, saying he has heard proof of it from Kunthi. Ruku retorts that the words of a prostitute aren't very trustworthy. Though Rukmani is rankled by Biswas's malicious suggestion, she calms herself, dismissing him as slippery and worthless.
- Then, Ruku goes to Kenny, bearing a welcoming garland and a lime for good luck. At Kenny's cottage Ruku suddenly feels embarrassed about her little gifts. Kenny's reception is cool, but the two soon fall into easy talk, punctuated with laughter and the occasional dark moment.

- Rukmani relates the deaths that have come with the hard times, and Kenny informs Ruku that his wife has left him, and his sons have been taught to forget him. Apparently, everyone has troubles. Ruku takes a moment to wrap her mind around how a wife could leave a husband, since her place to be beside him.
- The two then have a loaded symbolic talk about colonialism: India is Kenny's home, but not his home at all. Kenny is also confused about which is his country.
- Talk then turns to Ira, and we get the happy news that she's pregnant, but doesn't know who the father is. Kenny is unsurprised by the news of Ira's chosen career of streetwalking.
- Rukmani does a veiled and subtle job of defending her daughter's decision. She implies Ira's prostitution was only for the purpose of feeding Kuti. Furthermore, the girl was inexperienced in sexual matters, and got pregnant not knowing what she needed to do to guard against it.
- Kenny is philosophical about the matter: any baby, once it is born, must be loved, no matter what. Kenny insists that Ruku's shame about what people will say is foolish. On the walk home, Ruku ruminates on what Kenny says, as it is fairly similar to what Nathan thinks. A baby is a baby.

Chapter Nineteen

- Selvam, the last son with the family, comes home one day to announce that working the land is not for him. He has been patient with it, but the land doesn't take to him, nor he to the land. Rukmani is naturally worried about what Selvam will do to sustain himself after his parents are gone, but then comes the big news.
- Kenny is building a hospital, and he's invited Selvam to be his assistant. Selvam took to the little education he got from Ruku, and surpassed her learning through his own effort and enthusiasm. He reasons that he'll be a good assistant, and anything he doesn't know, Kenny will teach him.
- Mother and son then have a frank conversation. Selvam has already gotten his dad's good wishes to proceed with Kenny, but he hesitantly prods the question of whether his decision displeases his mother.
- She admits she's a bit disappointed, as his decision means none of their sons will go to the land that has been the mainstay of their parents' lives. Still, Rukmani assures Selvam she knows that this is the best thing for him.
- There's a moment of quiet recognition between the two of them: Rukmani pauses, wondering in her mind whether she should tell Selvam that people will talk, and say that Kenny's favor to Selvam is because of the "special relationship" Kenny has had with Selvam's mother. She decides not to say anything because she doesn't want to put a damper on his achievement and optimism.
- Selvam, though, is wise beyond his years. Without ever explicitly bringing up the rumor of Rukmani's infidelity, he assures his mother that he knows what gossip he might face, and he doesn't care. He insists that everything will be fine, so long as Rukmani keeps the strength to ignore such talk. Most importantly, Selvam says he trusts his mom. The two share a silent smile of understanding and relief that the topic has been addressed.

- Ruku then visits Kenny and thanks him for the favor to Selvam. Kenny shows her the plans for the new building—a big hospital, fit for the needs of the growing town. Rukmani doesn't quite grasp the details, but she gets that this is a big deal.
- She wonders where the money will come from the finance the thing, and Kenny announces that he has thousands of rupees. Rukmani is reasonably surprised, as Kenny has been living in poverty like the rest of the village people, but Kenny explains that the money isn't his. He's been raising funds from abroad and from within India.
- Then there's a big "meaning of life" talk – Ruku is puzzled at why people who don't know them would care enough to contribute money to a hospital to help the poor town.
- Kenny gets exasperated and goes into the old refrain that people who need help should cry out for it.
- Rukmani thinks to herself that this is foolish – man is given a spirit to rise above his needs. She thinks people should just accept want as a reality, and not ask for help from others.
- Though she doesn't speak a word of this, Kenny seems to sense that she's thinking it. He becomes irate as usual at the self-imposed suffering that he never can seem to understand. He argues that he doesn't grasp why the people around him seem to think of suffering as noble.
- Ruku counters that the people learn to bear suffering, as the priests have taught them to, and all of the suffering is central to cleansing the spirit.
- Kenny then proverbially throws up his hands, essentially admitting that he'll never understand the ways of the people around him.

Chapter Twenty

- It is time for Ira to give birth, and Rukmani prepares the house. She puts bamboo outside of the hut (a traditional warning to her husband and son that a birth is occurring in their one-room home). She cleans the house, puts down wet dung, and takes out the straw pallet women lie on to give birth, the same one she had used to give birth to Ira and all of her children.
- Rukmani then contemplates how many births the house has seen, and notes that this is the first that is not her own.
- As she thinks on it, she is plagued by doubts about the origin of Ira's baby. A man takes his wife gently, and watches over her in pregnancy, but when a baby is born out of wedlock, there is no guarantee that the baby will be clean, or the mother safe.
- Rukmani notes that Ira seems unperturbed by such concerns, and concludes that if she ever does worry, she wouldn't do it in front of her mother.
- Rukmani delivers Ira's baby, which confirms all of her fears about the strangeness of a baby born from a strange situation.
- Ira's baby is an albino, with white skin and pink eyes. She hands the baby to Ira and is shocked when Ira seems completely unfazed by the baby's oddity.
- Rukmani is confused: either Ira has gone mad, or her own pride as a mother gives her the strength to ignore the abnormality of the baby. She treats the baby as though it were perfect.
- Nathan is particularly perturbed by the whole affair, and he blames himself for letting this

happen. To him, the baby is wrong, and his weird physicality is a reflection of just how wrong the situation is.

- Rukmani tries to comfort him with the fact that Ira is OK with everything, but the parents dwell on the fact that the baby, with his sensitive albino eyes and skin, shrinks from the sunlight. The same happy sunlight that reared her children is a bane to this baby.
- The town gets news quickly of Ira's strange baby, and people come flooding in to see him as if he is a local curiosity. People are either sympathetic or they delight in the family's misery.
- Nathan finally can't take it anymore, and he declares they should have the traditional ceremony to name the child, which will remove all excuse for the "well-wishers" to make their visits of curiosity. On the tenth day after the birth, Old Granny arrives.
- The older woman gives a rupee to the baby, and Rukmani later learns it was her last. Old Granny blames herself for Ira's misfortune, because Ira's failed match was her doing.
- Rukmani realizes no one is to blame. Kenny has assured her that the fact that the baby is albino is not the fault of the father, but just a freak occurrence. Rukmani accepts that trying to lay blame is futile.
- It is when Kali finally comes to visit the baby that all of the concerns are blown open and put to rest. As Rukmani's most garrulous neighbor comes in to peer at the curiosity, Kali says what everyone has been thinking – the baby is simply not normal. Nathan is sour, Ira looks hurt, and everyone is silent and uncomfortable until Selvam puts them all to shame.
- Selvam is not even sixteen, but he is sensible. He declares that a pink-eyed baby is just as much a baby as a brown-eyed one. He chides Kali harshly, saying her own maternal instinct should have told her this.
- With this declaration made, he comforts the baby, who smiles at him. Kali, meanwhile, has slinks away, appropriately shamed by her own insensitivity.

Chapter Twenty-One

- Selvam becomes increasingly occupied with the building of the hospital, and Rukmani wistfully notes in retrospect that the hospital would take seven years to build, though none of them knew it at the time. Kenny and Selvam have poured their hearts into the project, and the delays leave them frustrated, though they plow on.
- Rukmani seems pained as she says if the hospital had been built faster, perhaps Old Granny would've had a decent place to die. She had lived on the street and died on the street, without relatives or anyone to care for her. The people of the town could see it happening, but it was easier to have a surface relationship than actually ask how the old lady was doing.
- Old Granny's body had been found outside, on a path near a well. She had died of starvation.
- Many from the town and village attended the cremation. Rukmani wryly notes that even if no one is there to take care of you in life, many show up for your death. Death removes the frightening responsibility that anyone might have had to take on for your ailing life.
- Rukmani takes Old Granny's death especially hard, as she knows now that the rupee Old Granny gave to Ira's baby, Sacrabani, was her last one. Nathan scolds her for being

foolish, as that one rupee wouldn't have held her long.

- Rukmani sadly wishes Old Granny could've gone to the hospital, but Nathan cuts her off sharply – hospitals are for the sick. For the old, there is nothing.
- The hospital carries other troubles besides building delays. Even as it is only being built, people begin to harass Kenny, Selvam, and even Ruku, trying to secure a spot once the facility opened. Rukmani is pained by the fact that not even a tenth of those seeking help can get it – there is just too much need. These fears go unspoken, and Ruku does the best she can.
- The building process is plagued by hiccoughs: the contractor is changed twice, alternating shortages of labor and materials, the theft of bricks, a fire, and inexplicable work stoppages. Kenny and Selvam are increasingly frustrated, and Ruku doesn't seem to know how to talk to either of them about what's going on.
- Finally, Ruku talks to Selvam and learns that when Kenny goes away, he's still collecting money for the project.
- Rukmani again marvels at what she sees as foolishness. There is no purse big enough, not enough compassion in the world, to help all those who are in need. She concludes Kenny is wrong for his optimism in people. She doesn't understand how Kenny and Selvam manage to fund the project, but the work always seems to crawl on anyway.
- Ultimately, Selvam begins his actual training with Kenny in Kenny's whitewashed little cottage. Selvam picks up quickly, and by his second year he's able to treat less complicated cases himself. Kenny begins to pay Selvam a small wage when he can. Rukmani one day questions Kenny about how he will manage to pay a full staff, but Kenny is brash and darkly hopeful. He is certain he will find ways and means.

Chapter Twenty-Two

- The family operates in strange ways. Rukmani notes that Ira and Selvam have always been close, and Ira has always treated Selvam more as her own son than just another brother. It seems that as the children have gotten older, they have become distant from their parents, but never from each other. Kali, ever helpful, suggests that it is because the children are better educated than their parents, but it seems to really be something deeper than that.
- It's particularly notable that Selvam has always loved Ira's baby, whom he treats as totally normal. Nonetheless, Rukmani describes how such a charade is doomed to failure. Sacrabani does not play with the other children, because their games are in the sun, which hurts him. He looks strange, his reactions to being outside are pitiable, but he endures the stares of children and adults alike.
- Finally, one day Sacrabani confronts Ira with the inevitable question about what it means to be a bastard. Ira is blind-sided, she can only imagine how much he knows, or what inspired him to ask this question. She flounders before explaining that bastards are children who are unwanted, and his mother loves him dearly. Still, Ruku notes Ira's voice is pained, as she tells us Ira had indeed sought an abortion early in her pregnancy.
- Ira is again discomfited when later, Sacrabani asks if he has a father. Ira is startled, but quickly says of course he has a father, but his father is away, and will visit when he can. Ira

delivers the standard "you'll understand when you're older," and shoos Sacrabani out to play.

- Left alone with their daughter, Ruku helpfully offers that she would've said Sacrabani's father was dead, so as to end all the questionings. Nathan is gentler, saying it is for Ira to deal with the matter as she sees fit. Ira is clearly hurt, though, and counters that the boy is only a baby. She thinks he wouldn't understand such complicated matters as death. It's clear these questions are being fed to him from the outside.
- Ira wanders outside of the hut, and they decide it's best to let her do her own thing for a while. Eventually, though, Nathan goes to his daughter. Moved by his gentleness, it seems Ira is finally comfortable enough to cry. Ruku hears her weep for a long time.

Chapter Twenty-Three

- We learn that Murugan, the son who had gone away to a city to work as a servant, has married. Ruku and Nathan could not afford to attend the wedding, but more importantly, Nathan was too sick to make the trip.
- Nathan is approaching 50, and is plagued by rheumatism and fevers that leave him increasingly weak. As a result, Nathan is unable to work the land. Though Ira and Rukmani try as they can to tend to the earth, they cannot make as much of an impact as Nathan did.
- Kenny cares for Nathan, and tells Ruku that the man hasn't been eating well enough. Rukmani points out that they eat as well as they can.
- Kenny also thinks that Nathan worries too much, which only makes him weaker. Rukmani says he is right to worry, as his whole family depends on him for their livelihood. She immediately regrets saying this to Kenny, as she doesn't want to seem selfish. Ruku acknowledges, though, that this is the truth, and even Kenny cannot deny that.
- Talk then turns to whether Ruku's many sons can support the family. Rukmani notes that her sons have made their lives elsewhere, and almost instantly, Kenny crumbles. He knows he has taken the last of Rukmani's sons from her, and he is stricken by it. Still, Rukmani assures him that she wants for Selvam what Selvam wants for himself.
- Kenny asks Rukmani if she never plans for the future, and she gently points out the obvious. Under conditions like these, no plans can be made. Rukmani declares that they are all in God's hands.
- Before long, Nathan begins to get better, almost miraculously.
- Then, everything takes a turn for the worse.
- Rukmani comes home one day to find Sacrabani cowering in a corner, looking with terror and curiosity at his grandfather, who is sitting on the floor gazing into nothingness. Rukmani thinks Nathan has just had one of his attacks again, and she gives him water to drink, tending to him gently.
- Nathan then announces the worst news of all: Sivaji has paid a surprise visit, and their land is to be sold to the tannery. The thirty years they've spent on the land doesn't matter because the tannery will pay more. What's more: the deal has already been completed and the family only has two weeks left.
- Rukmani is naturally in shock, and wonders where they'll go, and what they'll do. She finally admits that they are surrounded by mad chaos.

- Rukmani and Nathan are both in shock, and they distractedly discuss what on earth the tannery will do with this little land that is only good for rice growing. Rukmani helpfully the fact that at least they won't have to carry much, in consolation.
- Rukmani then wanders into her own thoughts about the tannery, declaring that she always knew it would be their ruin. Some have benefited from it, no doubt, but many more have suffered, it seems. Her family once had prosperity from the tannery, but those days seem to have long since passed.
- Rukmani then pauses in her reflection to admit that the tannery is not entirely to blame. The land is a fickle thing, and people who make their living on it must live with the uncertainty that there will be times of plenty, and times of nothingness, glut and dearth in equal parts, both equally impossible to anticipate.
- With the land gone, Rukmani knows they have nothing. She walks into the hut, and surveys the long history of what has happened there.
- Selvam comes home later that night, and when Nathan breaks the news to him, he is thoughtfully silent. Rukmani has a moment of weakness and wonders whether Selvam's silence is because he does not care. She immediately remembers Selvam is a quiet, thoughtful man and quickly is ashamed of herself.
- When Selvam finally speaks, he is furious. Like his brothers before him, he has an acute sense of justice, and he declares that it is simply not right that the tannery should do this.
- His parents are more pliable to bad fates, choosing not to shake their fists at heaven in futility. Nathan declares they will go to Murugan in the city. He's too old now to be able to guarantee hard work and profit – no one would sell land to him under that kind of uncertainty. Rukmani's optimism rails against Nathan's harsh words, but he insists that they are true, and must be said.
- Nathan comforts Rukmani, and in a tender moment, he lays his hands on her temples. It becomes clear to her that they suffer for each other more than for themselves. It might be easier to not have to worry about each other, but they couldn't bear their other worries if they didn't have each other.
- Rukmani's head is unclear, and she leaves the practical arrangements of their future to her husband and son.
- Rukmani breaks out of her blurred thinking when she hears Selvam speak. In a profound moment of self-sacrifice, Selvam offers to return to the land. He and his father can work it together, and perhaps they might live as they once did. Nathan brightens for a moment at the prospect, but his generosity matches his son's. He knows what he would be taking away from Selvam by putting him back on the land, and Nathan's final verdict is that Selvam should pursue his hospital work.
- Then there is the question of Ira and Sacrabani. Though Nathan and Rukmani are sure they must go, Ira declares she and her son have a home here, as uncomfortable as it may be. People are used to her and her strange son, and she does not want to start a new life somewhere else.
- Selvam vows to care for Ira and Sacrabani, though it pains him that he has nothing to give his parents. Taking care of his sister and nephew is the best gesture he can offer.
- It is settled that Selvam will take care of her and her son. In the end, it is decided that only Nathan and Rukmani will go, leaving behind what's left of their family.

Chapter Twenty-Four

- Faced with leaving, Rukmani begins to collect the few belongings they plan to take with them. She packs their sleeping mats, a little food, and two bowls. Then she begins to survey the implements of the kitchen that she cannot bring.
- Wistfully, she notes that her cooking days are over, and she thinks fondly of the daily rituals of food preparation in which she will no longer participate. The journey to Murugan and his wife will take two days, so she takes the proper supplies: bellows for the fire and six dung cakes, (for cooking fuel on the journey).
- Rukmani goes to the granary and digs up the bundle of money that is left. It's sixteen rupees total, three of their own, three from Selvam, and a ten-rupee note sent from Kenny.
- The bullock cart arrives in the morning (already packed with skins from the tannery), and Nathan and Rukmani climb in. Selvam, Ira, and Sacrabani see the cart off. Nathan and Rukmani look back at all they're leaving behind. The journey is long and dusty, and Nathan and Rukmani are comforted by each other.
- Finally, on the second day, the driver of the cart announces he has taken them as far as he can. Rukmani and Nathan are a little daunted: they are faced with three roads and have no idea how to find their son. They choose a road at random and trust they'll find their son with the kindness of strangers' directions.
- When they finally run into somebody who can direct them, they hear the bad news that the street they're looking for, Koil street, is some fifteen miles away. They are crest-fallen, but they have no choice except to continue. While they walk, many carts pass them. No one offers them a ride, though, because the carts are already full.
- Nathan and Rukmani are growing weary of their bundles, which seem to get heavier. They stop frequently to marvel at how busy and bustling the city is. There are people and traffic far greater than they'd ever seen.
- Finally, they reach the city center, and, knowing Koil Street is still some six miles away, they stop to rest. After a light meal of plantains, darkness falls around them, and they know they have stayed too long. A man they saw sleeping in a doorway earlier tells them that they can go to a nearby temple for food and a place to sleep. Rukmani and Nathan are buoyed by the prospect of some proper rest.
- The temple complex is bustling, and it seems the temple is a familiar place to many others who are also heading there for food and shelter. The atmosphere is jovial and familiar enough for the people who are used to it. Nathan and Rukmani chat with the other pilgrims, eagerly talking of visiting their son, though no one has heard of him.
- The couple arrives at the inner part of the temple, and they stop to pray in a service led by two priests. During the service, Rukmani is distracted. As she tries to focus on her prayers, all she can see are the images of her past: her children, her hut, Old Granny, Kenny, Sacrabani. Finally, her mind calms, and she prays amid the reverent silence.
- The atmosphere of the place entirely changes once the prayers are over. The people for whom this is a nightly routine know that the food offerings placed before the gods and goddesses in the temple are given to the poor after the food is blessed. There is a throng of people who push and jostle for a place in the line for handouts.
- Rukmani makes it into the crush, but Nathan, who has never been one for crowds, stands to the side with the old and crippled. She thinks she can ask for her husband's portion to be given to her, but when she finally makes it to the front of the line, she is sharply rebuked

for asking for a second portion. The people who hand out food chastise her for "making capital of charity," and in the end Rukmani walks away with only one portion to share between her and Nathan.

- Still, it's good to have food. After she and Nathan have eaten, they contentedly feed the temple goats the banana leaf plates and cups that held their evening's meal. Only then do they remember their bundles, which they've forgotten in the temple.
- Along with a small party of helpers, they search for the bundles in vain. They know it was foolish to leave the bundles unattended, but they aren't accustomed to the city, where nothing is safe.
- Though they resign themselves to their loss, Rukmani is terribly uneasy – she will go to her daughter-in-law like a beggar without so much as a cooking pot. She decides she will spend a little of their money on wares to bring to her daughter-in-law, and she settles into an uneasy sleep. While sleeping, she's awakened twice by the feeling that fingers are tugging at her arms and face. The first time, she thinks it's only Nathan, but the second time, she finds she cannot go back to sleep.
- Awake in the dark, she marvels at the statues in the temples. They almost seem to move, and only with the falling light of the dawn does it seem that the figures return to their carved stillness.

Chapter Twenty-Five

- Nathan awakes from a good sleep. He notes how it seems Rukmani has had a harder time getting rest. They set off, but it's not long before Nathan is eyeing up all the savory food being sold from the stalls. They know it's a splurge, but Nathan thinks they should spend a little money on food.
- Rukmani resolves to buy something to eat, and only when she reaches for the pouch tied into her waistband does she realize the money is gone.
- They return to the temple to look for the money on the floor where they slept, but it is not there. A few people in the temple recognize them from the last night and cruelly tease them that free food is only given in the evening, not the morning too. When they hear of the stolen money, they soften a little, but the general consensus is that this is the usual stuff that happens in the city. Their money is definitely gone, and they have only the clothes on their back.
- Nathan and Rukmani steel themselves from hunger enough to continue their journey. Since the city is a big and confusing place, they feel utterly lost and are constantly misdirected.
- Finally, they stop to rest at a roadside, where they watch about a dozen street children at play. The children are merry in spite of their apparent malnourishment.
- Though they play enough like children, they turn into animals when a scrap of bread is dropped, snarling and scrapping amongst each other for the smallest morsel. When they see rich men, they become beggars, knowing the wiles of what the street requires.
- Rukmani can't help but compare these street urchins to her children. Though she knows that her own children have been this hungry, she feels comfort that her children acted quite like this.

- After watching a while, Nathan suggests they ask one of the street-smart kids for directions. They find one who explains that there are actually three or four Koil Streets (hence all the confusion). The little boy is able to work off of the detail that Murugan works for a well-known man named Birla. Though he doesn't know Murugan, he says he'll take Nathan and Rukmani to Birla. If they prosper there, they can pay him for his trouble.
- The little boy announces that he is called Puli ("lion"), after the king of the animals. He says he is well known, and from the way he deals with the other children, it's clear that he's the leader of the pack. For all his confidence and impudence, Nathan and Ruku find something really appealing about this clever boy, who could well be one of their own grand-children.
- Only then do they notice that the boy has stumps where his fingers should be. He is diseased leprosy, which will continue to eat away at his body. Puli leads them to a street with a whitewashed house and church, and he tells them that this is the end of their journey.
- Some servant men come to shoo away Nathan and Rukmani, whom they take for beggars. Nathan explains that he's looking for his son Murugan, only to learn that no one living there has that name. With no further information, the servants try to rush away the couple, especially as the doctor is just arriving back to the house.
- Nathan has not come so far to turn back now, and he insists he'll speak to the doctor. To Nathan and Rukmani's surprise, the doctor is a woman. She remembers Murugan, and asks for news of their village hospital and Kenny (who sent Murugan to her in the first place).
- Sadly, though, she tells them that Murugan hasn't worked for her for two years. She senses their desperation and says that he was a good worker, but that he went to seek higher wages working for the well-known Collector, who lives on Chamundi Hill. She promises anyone can direct them there.
- Rukmani and Nathan are at the gate, about to continue on this harrowing journey, when the doctor calls them back. She can tell they look hungry, and she invites them to have a meal. They are taken to the servants' quarters by a manservant, named Das, and he brings them to a woman (presumably his wife) who is busy preparing a meal.
- The young woman is nursing a chubby baby, and she warms immediately to Nathan and Rukmani, hearing that they are the parents of the one whom her husband replaced. For Rukmani, the woman's kindness is a breath of fresh air, and the old couple is comforted for the first time in a long while.
- They wash up, and Ruku fills us on in the filthiness of the latrine (a thing she has never used before). This bathroom doesn't provide the cleanliness of nature alone. Nathan tells her she'll have to get used to things being like this in city life.
- Back at the cooking pot, the rosy young woman holds the baby on her hip, and she introduces three more babies. Ruku holds the baby, a little girl, as the woman scoops out generous portions of rice for her guests.
- The woman informs the couple that they are given free rice and dhal from the doctor, and the doctor has sent her extra on account of the unexpected company. Ruku eats happily, especially once she knows she's not taking food from a family that already had so many little mouths to feed. Das's wife is so kind that she convinces Nathan and Ruku to spend the night, and sleeping mats are soon spread out for them.
- They leave in the morning after thanking the lady doctor, as well as Das and his wife. Ruku says when she thinks of Das's wife now, she sees her just as then, surrounded by her children, sunny and warm, a bit of comfort in an unfamiliar world.

Chapter Twenty-Six

- Nathan and Rukmani go to the Collector's house on Chamundi Hill in search of their son. It's a fine and beautiful house, but as the old couple approach, a man immediately runs out to shoo them away, taking them for beggars.
- They announce they are not beggars, but have come to look for their son, Murugan. Hearing this, the man immediately softens, and brusquely delivers them to Murugan's wife's godown before rushing off. (A "godown" is a tiny section of a warehouse that can be used as a home.)
- Murugan's wife's dwelling (one small square room set in a long row of similar rooms) is not too different from the one Das and his family kept.
- At the threshold, Rukmani and Nathan hesitate, overcome with excitement and a kind of shyness. They think about being reunited with their son, whom they haven't seen for so long, and finally meeting his wife, whom they've never known. They can't quite bring themselves to step into the door, so they call for Murugan's wife from the threshold.
- A thin girl with "untidy hair" answers them at the door, and their reception is shockingly cold. She wants to know who they are and what they want. Once more, Ruku is embarrassed that she and Nathan must look like beggars. Nathan explains that they aren't beggars at all, but Murugan's parents.
- Hearing this, the woman, (we find out that her name is "Ammu"), lets them in, but she looks strangely uncertain about what to do with them. It turns out her discomfort stems from the fact that Murugan has left her. He's been gone two years, and she safely assumes that he isn't coming back.
- Of course, Nathan and Rukmani are shocked – they've come this far for nothing. It's clear the girl is struggling on her own just to feed the two babies she has. There's no way she'll be able to take care of them too.
- Her demeanor with them is cold, likely because she understands that they came to get help. Ammu seems accusatory of the old couple. Ruku understands this coldness because the blame is partly theirs: had they raised him better, he would not have deserted this woman and his child.
- Ammu announces that she'll be going off to do her work (cleaning houses) but Nathan and Rukmani can stay until she gets back to reach the children. The baby she has on her hip begins to cry as soon as she puts him down. Ruku wants to hold him to see if he'll quiet down.
- Ammu is fine with that, but she adds sharply that Rukmani should know the child is not her grandchild. She defensively says "One must live," expecting Ruku to have some scolding for her, but of course Ruku doesn't. (It seems Ammu, driven by hunger like Ira, turned to giving away her body for money. The baby must be less than two years old, and was thus conceived after Murugan left.)
- Ammu returns from cleaning houses (where she earns fifteen rupees a month and gets free housing) at midday, and Rukmani can tell that she and Nathan were not really supposed to take up Ammu's invitation that they stay for a meal.
- Their meal is made with half-hostility. It's clear the girl has some concern for what will happen to these old people, and where they'll go, but she can't take on their burden in

addition to her own. The sooner they leave her, the better.

- As Nathan explains that they'll be on their way back to the village, he qualifies that they only came to the city for their son. There's added awkwardness as Rukmani tries weakly to defend Murugan's desertion, saying he must have had some reason. Ammu is infuriated by this, and says Murugan only left to chase women and gambling.
- Nathan diffuses the tension a little by assuring Ammu that they'll go back to their son and daughter in the village. He worries for her though: she will face one challenge after another as a young woman fending for herself and two babies. Ammu is cold in her replies – she's sure she can take care of herself and her children just fine. Rukmani can tell the girl has been hardened, and can anticipate that Ammu will only receive more challenges.
- There's only so long one can hang around in awkwardness and hostility, even when one has no place to go, so soon enough Nathan and Rukmani leave.
- Rukmani notes that the parting is sad, even though the meeting was a bit weird. She's saddened by the prospect that she'll likely never see this daughter-in-law and these children again.
- Lost in their thoughts, Rukmani and Nathan wander to the wrong exit. One of the servants screams behind them that they're supposed to use the servant's exit, and they should remember that for next time. Nathan (who still has his usual gracious dignity) replies that they are not servants, and there will be no next time.

Chapter Twenty-Seven

- After their disappointing encounter with Ammu, Nathan and Rukmani return to the temple. The regulars among the destitute have mixed reactions, grumbling that the city temple should feed its own poor without having to cater to all of India's poor. The harsh reality is that each new arrival means a little less food for the others.
- Soon enough, Nathan and Rukmani become regulars themselves. They grow accustomed to the cruelties that make the temple-goers competitors: crippled people have their crutches kicked from under them, and the weak are separated from their supporters so there's more food to go around for those who can stand the crush of the line.
- In all of this, Rukmani often has to get a single portion and share it with Nathan, as he does not adapt well to the temple crowds.
- As each night descends, Nathan and Ruku plan their journey back to their village. If they're going to live in destitution, it might as well be in the place they call home. Still, they have no money to make the journey.
- Rukmani then has the idea that she can make a little money using her education as a reader and writer of letters. This opportunity gives the old couple some hope.
- Still, Rukmani is a woman, and people in the city often stop to marvel at her as she sets up shop in the market. A literate woman is an unusual thing. Business isn't terribly good, but Ruku earns enough for them to eat rice cakes in the mornings.
- It's a new year, and Nathan and Ruku find themselves still living in homeless poverty in the city. Nathan's rheumatism has begun to act up again, and they become increasingly desperate to return home.
- One day, as Rukmani returns to the temple from the marketplace, a little boy calls after

her. It's none other than Puli, the street child who gave helped them find Murugan. Puli speaks like a man, and Ruku still finds him charming. He demands payment for his past service to Rukmani, and to show him that she has nothing she takes him to the temple with her.

- There, Puli shares the single portion of dinner with Rukmani and Nathan, and to Ruku's surprise, he also nestles next to them to sleep. Ruku worries that he should go home to his mother, but he tells her he has no home, and no mother to worry about him.

- Rukmani knows this street-smart boy is perfectly fine on his own. She worries for him, though she lacks the resources to take care of him herself. Still, Nathan echoes her practical concern when he chides Ruku that they can't add the boy to their burden, whether he is "whole" of body or not.

- In the morning, though, Puli shows he can earn his keep. He tells them about a nearby stone quarry where anyone can work. They can break small rocks off the big stones, and will be paid by the sack, earning much more than Ruku is currently making as a letter writer. Puli can't do it himself because he can't hold a hammer, (he has lost fingers as a result of his leprosy). Still, he'll direct their work.

- Puli leads Nathan and Ruku to the quarry. It's hard work, and noisy, especially when the sheet rock is exploded into smaller bits by gunpowder, as is often done. Nathan and Rukmani don't have hammers, and are not as experienced as the other workers at using stones to chip off other stones.

- Puli sits and watches them, but he comes in handy when he rescues them from their own distraction. The hoisting of a red flag signals impending explosions at the quarry, and Puli once pulls Nathan and Ruku to safety away from the blast when they don't notice the flag. This ragged threesome has become something of a team.

- After their first day's work, Rukmani has a bit of difficulty figuring out exactly how the payment process works. As she's in line waiting to present her stones, she sees that Puli has brought out a begging bowl, and changed his voice, asking onlookers to take pity on this orphaned leper.

- When she finally presents her and Nathan's basket of stones to the overseer, she gets eight annas, which amounts to four times what she made in a day at the market. Suddenly, going home to the village seems something of a possibility.

- Puli, Nathan, and Ruku set up a routine of sorts: working at the quarry and sleeping at the temple. Though Puli is wily, Ruku entrusts their money to him, as he's far more able to take care of it than either of them are. Calculating what they might make at the quarry, they figure that they could return home within two months.

- In this excited planning, Nathan asks Puli if he'll come with them to the village. Puli reminds them that the city is his home – he knows the place like the back of his hand, and has made a name for himself here.

- Besides, Puli chides, if Nathan and Ruku are returning to poverty in their village, he might as well enjoy the poverty he already knows in the city. He's happy to live just as he did before the old couple arrived.

- Still, Rukmani begins to worry about what will happen to Puli when the leprosy that took his fingers begins to claim other parts of his body, making him increasingly disabled. She respects Puli's independence, and appreciates that he puts up with their dependence on him. Still, she knows there are limitations as to what one can do under miserable circumstances.

Chapter Twenty-Eight

- It was a particularly good day at the quarry, and Nathan and Ruku managed to earn one whole rupee. Rukmani is elated, they've already earned six, and their journey back to their village seems to be closer than ever.
- There is a pleasant drizzle as the three walk back from the quarry. Nathan says he is tired, so he'll go ahead to the temple, but Rukmani and Puli go to the bazaar to buy the usual rice cakes.
- The vendor Rukmani usually buys rice cakes from is kind to her (even though she can't buy much) and he sometimes even gives her a little butter for the cakes. He's happy for Ruku's little extra earnings when she announces today she might be able to buy some more than usual.
- Ruku and Puli eye all of the delicacies they usually avoid looking at, and they finally settle on buying fried pancakes, spending ten annas (more than a usual day's earning) on pancakes and rice cakes.
- On the walk home, Ruku and Puli spot a hawker selling little pull carts carrying drums. Puli is enamored of the toys, and he begs Ruku to stop and watch them for a bit.
- The hawker is smooth-tongued, and Puli is desperate, so before long he's convinced Rukmani to spend two annas on the cart for him.
- Rukmani softens when she remembers he is only a little boy, and he's had a hard life. As thoughts of home have been on her mind, she adds one more extravagance, deciding to buy a cart for her grandson, Sacrabani too. She thinks of how it will excite him, and make Ira smile.
- In the end, Ruku is left with two pull-carts, pancakes, rice cakes, and only two annas for the day's work. She's panicking in her mind over how to explain this wastefulness to Nathan, but when she sees him she realizes there are bigger problems to address.
- Rukmani tries to present the pancakes to Nathan with fake cheer, but already he's looking ill. When he returns from vomiting, Nathan says seeing the food made his stomach turn. He admits he's been sick and feverish since the morning.
- They eat the rice cakes in silence. As the rain gets heavier and Nathan's chill worsens, Rukmani tries to convince him to stay out of the rain at the temple. Nathan refuses to stay behind, because the rain is likely to go on for days and he doesn't want to miss work. In the end, he goes to the quarry with them, still sick.
- The quarry is a big muddy wet mess. While the wealthier people could afford slickers to cover themselves, Nathan and Ruku are exposed to the downpour. It's been seven days of continuous rain. Even when Puli decides he won't go to the quarry, Nathan insists on going to work in the bare hillside in the pouring rain beside Rukmani.
- One rainy day, without Puli, Nathan, and Ruku are at the quarry, and dusk is falling. Nathan tells Ruku she should go collect their day's pay, while he goes home without her. Ruku, left on her own, can't keep thoughts of home out of her head. She wonders whether home will still be there, and wonders wistfully whether Puli will stay behind after all.
- Rukmani then stumbles down the wet hillside, and halfway down she notes a small crowd of people. At first she ignores it, until one of the crowd calls out to her that she must come see to her husband, who has fallen.

- Rukmani's senses leave her for a moment, but she's soon by Nathan's side. He's been carried to the side of the road, where he's lying in the mud, jerking, twitching, and breathing hoarsely. His body is cold to the touch.
- It continues to rain mercilessly, and Ruku tries to pull off some of her sari to cover him, but it gives way to her touch, as it is so old. No others have anything to lend Nathan to cover himself – they are all in equally pitiful circumstances. Finally, two men begin carrying Nathan to the temple, hoisting him by his arms and legs. A knot of women follow behind with Ruku, saying comforting things, but Ruku is so distracted and numb that it's as if nothing is said at all.
- Only when Ruku licks her lips from the rainwater does she realize that she's been crying.

Chapter Twenty-Nine

- Rukmani makes an unusual switch from the past tense of the narrative here, and recounts her feelings in the present. She remembers this particular night in painfully meticulous detail, and recounts it to her reader.
- As the men carried Nathan's shivering body to the temple, Ruku follows behind and notices that the insistent rain has squelched the flame usually burning on top of the temple. Rukmani remembers crying out repeatedly like a madwoman, "Fire cannot burn in water."
- The men lay Nathan down on the pavement of the temple, and Rukmani sinks down at his side. Someone brings them a lamp, someone brings them water, and Ruku wipes down Nathan's mud-caked body. Finally, it's just Nathan and Ruku alone. The helpers all slip away as they begin to see the inevitable.
- Nathan lies with his head in Ruku's lap, and he twitches, muttering about his sons. Ruku evaluates the sad state of his feverish, skinny body. His mind is also beginning to slip into delirium.
- His senses seem to return to him momentarily at midnight. He reaches out and touches Ruku's face, wiping away her tears with his hand and telling her, "What has to be, has to be."
- Rukmani is defiant, and tries to tell Nathan that he'll get better. But Nathan knows it isn't true. He tells her not to force him to stay, now that it's his time. He also tells her not to grieve.
- Rukmani points out that she doesn't grieve for him. She fears that she cannot live on after him: he is her love and her life.
- Nathan tries to comfort her, and says he will live on his children. They share an incredibly poignant moment as Nathan reminds Rukmani that they have been very happy together. With her face laid on his, Rukmani listens to his soft breathing, until he turns his face towards her and dies.

Chapter Thirty

- Without much detail, Rukmani tells us how she strove to pull together the pieces of her life,

but Nathan's absence continues to loom.

- For comfort from loneliness, she turns to Puli. She makes promises about his health, saying his condition would improve if he returned to her village with her. Puli eases her pain gradually, and eventually he decides to come home with her.
- Rukmani glosses over the bullock cart ride home, and she tells us seeing the land is life to her starving spirit. She weeps from happiness, and the hard past begins to drop away from her.
- Selvam and Ira both run out to greet her. Puli stands to the side, clutching his pull-cart with the drum. She calls to him, and shows him to Selvam and Ira, announcing that he too is her son, as she and Nathan adopted him.
- Ira immediately takes Puli's arm, and tells him to come with her. She says he looks hungry, and tells him he should rest while she prepares some rice.
- Ira and Puli walk ahead, while Ruku stays back with Selvam, struggling to say the unutterable. Selvam assures her they'll manage, and sensing her difficulty, he tells his mother she doesn't need to talk about what happened.
- Ruku tells her son Nathan's passing was gentle, and that she'll tell him about it later.
- And on that look towards the future

Themes

Theme of Life, Consciousness, and Existence

The meaning of life is constantly questioned and probed in this text. Life means different things to different characters: For Rukmani, it is an opportunity for endurance and spiritual cleansing through suffering; for Nathan, life is about finding little joys and simple pleasures. Kenny's life is about helping those who suffer, regardless of the cost to one's self. Life's meaning is a dynamic thing, and it changes with circumstances. When harvests are good, life is not hard, and so it isn't thought about that often. When things are bad though, there is always an opportunity to reckon with the reality that one must go on, and that life must have some innate value that makes it worth living. The characters struggle and find that meaning, each in their own way.

Questions About Life, Consciousness, and Existence

1. Ruku describes "hope and fear" as the twin forces that rule her life. Is one more important than the other? Does Ruku really seem inspired by hope, or does she hint that hope is a pacifying salve that she uses because she has no other alternative, except futile despair?
2. Is the religious belief that suffering brings spiritual cleansing the driving force of Ruku's hopeful life? Does Ruku ever rail against the gods for her lifelong suffering?
3. Does Rukmani think she's had a good life? What rubric is used to measure a good life in the book?
4. How does the meaning of life differ between generations? Compare the lives of Old Granny, Ruku and Nathan, and Ruku and Nathan's children.

Chew on Life, Consciousness, and Existence

Rukmani is different from her children in that she does not view life as a dynamic learning experience. (12.23) Ruku has a firm view on the meaning of life, based on her cultural and spiritual values. Her children, by contrast, adjust their view on the meaning of life based on what's going on circumstantially in their lives.

Each person's view on the meaning of life is shaped by their social status in life – Kenny has the luxury of pity, Kunthi's life is defined by her dissatisfaction as a woman of the earth, and Ruku accepts being a plain village woman.

Theme of Suffering

Suffering is fact of life in *Nectar in a Sieve*. Characters suffer financially, but they also suffer in deeper and more personal ways. Rukmani watches as her children starve, and her family breaks apart. She even holds her husband as he dies. There's a message that suffering, because it is a natural part of life, must be borne. There's also a lot of interesting discussion between Kenny and Rukmani about whether suffering can be fought. These characters question whether there's any purpose in being angry about the injustice of suffering if there's nothing they can do about it. Ultimately they come down on different sides. Rukmani accepts suffering, while her last son devotes his life to trying to alleviate it. Suffering brings spiritual cleansing, but it also inspires people to hope that there is something beyond suffering.

Questions About Suffering

1. Nathan suggests the landowner could only really enjoy the fruits of his business by ignoring all the suffering his business causes. Is it true that people can't really enjoy the profits of other people's suffering? If people were really exposed to the suffering of others, would they feel forced to do something about it?
2. Which is the greater cause of suffering: the things the characters can't control, like the weather and the harvests – or the things they can, like the way they think of themselves and treat each other?
3. Of the many challenges Nathan has faces, which represents the greatest blow? Is losing the land the one thing that really pitches him into suffering, or is there more to the story?
4. Ruku tells Kenny that suffering in silence cleanses the soul, and that she will ultimately be rewarded for her suffering. Does Ruku really believe this? Are there other indications, times she falters in the face of suffering, or lashes out, that tell us she's not so stoic and passive as she originally appears?

Chew on Suffering

Though Rukmani purports throughout the novel to have a system of beliefs that appreciates the meaning and value of suffering, the greater thrust of the novel suggests that the author, Markandaya, may actually believe the amount of suffering in the story to be needless.

Theme of Transformation

Transformation has many facets in *Nectar in a Sieve*. Characters are transformed by hardship, learning how to endure and transcend difficulties. The town is transformed by the tannery, which disrupts caste traditions and the environment. The world is becoming modern and industrial, a change from rural and agricultural. Characters' values change when faced with the reality of what poverty drives people to do (prostitution, thievery, etc), and their own hopes for themselves are gently dimmed and often redirected throughout the novel. Change is inevitable, and the story directs its focus toward watching people grow and adapt to the world as it changes around them. They have no choice but to transform if they are to survive, and this transformation occurs socially, but also personally.

Questions About Transformation

1. As narrator, Rukmani has control over the shape of her own story, but do we get any indications from her about how she's changed throughout the story, if at all?
2. In what ways does the tannery transform the town? Is it *forcing* people and customs to change, as Ruku might argue, or is it just giving people some opportunity to try something new, which they were looking for anyway?
3. Is it important that this novel be happening in the mid-20th century, a time of great change in India? Are the transformations going on (both external and internal for the characters) better understood before the backdrop of post-independence India, or could these changes be happening at any time, regardless of political circumstances?
4. Ira changes from a loving and obedient daughter to a prostitute, and back again, through the course of the novel. What prompts these changes?
5. Do Ira's transformations reflect at all on the changing role of women in India, or are the changes purely a product of Ira's personal circumstances?

Chew on Transformation

It's not India's political situation alone that changes in the book, it's the Indians themselves. Note that all Nathan and Ruku's children do exactly the opposite of what's expected of them, and their parents are powerless to do anything about it. The book is about changes that were occurring with the new generation of Indians, as India was going through its own national growing pains.

Rukmani has changed over the course of the story; the woman she describes at the start of the novel is young and flush with hope. The reason the book is so focused on suffering and failure is because Ruku, retrospectively, realized those things were the greatest influences in her life, and they've changed her into a resigned (but content) old woman.

Theme of Man and the Natural World

Nature is a dual force in the novel. It brings great joy but also great pain. Characters often get angry about other forces beyond their control (the tannery, their children). However, for all the grief they get from nature, they never come to resent this powerful force. One of the greatest

philosophical points of the book is that nature reflects the arbitrary beauty and suffering inherent in life. One can only appreciate what there is to appreciate, and endure what must be endured. Though nature often hurts her, in the end it is the thing for which she endures, knowing that it too endures and will last long after her.

Questions About Man and the Natural World

1. How does Rukmani maintain her love of nature in spite of all the hardships it brings her? Is Rukmani just being delusional or overly sentimental about her love of the land? Is she ignoring how cruel the land has been to them?
2. How is nature symbolic in this novel? Is it a representation of the rebirth central to human hope? Is it just what it is, an inevitable but predictable changing cycle, and nothing more?
3. How is nature tied into one's spiritual, moral, and personal development in the novel?
4. Might Rukmani's disdain for the city come from the circumstances under which she's in the city, rather than an innate dislike for the city itself?
5. If Rukmani can romanticize nature so much, why can her children not do the same?

Chew on Man and the Natural World

Nature is a cruel force, but it stands in contrast to the even more cruel force of urban modernity, which destroys the environment and the traditions of India. Within this paradigm, for all its challenges, nature is definitely the lesser of two evils.

Theme of Poverty

Poverty is the everyday reality of the characters in the novel. Poverty is not an abstract concept that one can really think about; it's like a wolf at the door that must constantly be staved off. Poverty is so dire in this novel that characters don't have the luxury to ruminate on it. Instead, they build their lives around the knowledge that it will always haunt them, and the best they can do is try to keep afloat. Poverty is definitely always present, but one of the strengths of *Nectar in a Sieve* is that it need not always be the focus. The novel gives us a rare glimpse into the complex lives and emotions people live (even when they are in poverty). Characters are driven by it, but it is not all that shapes them. They cannot financially transcend it, but they learn to define themselves spiritually beyond it.

Questions About Poverty

1. Does Rukmani ever feel guilty for bringing her children into a situation of poverty? Does she see herself as responsible for their suffering, or does she think it is something they should all bear through together? (Think of her response to Arjun's complaint that there isn't enough to eat, or Selvam's calmness at hearing the land had been sold.)
2. Does Rukmani take poverty for granted? Does she resent it, or does she appreciate it in a weird way? Is Rukmani's view akin to a shtick from a Dickens novel, where poverty becomes a gauge of moral goodness and personal humility?
3. Is the poverty in this novel realistic? Can we relate to he characters relatable, or is their

experience with poverty, starvation, and displacement too far from our own experiences for us to be empathic? If one does not relate or sympathize with the plight of the poverty-stricken, does the book still resonate?

4. The Indian characters in the book don't seem to back each other up, though they all suffer from poverty. (Think of Ruku's refusal to help Janaki or even Old Granny.) Kenny, on the other hand, has devoted his own life to helping the Indians get out of poverty and suffering, even though his convictions have put him into poverty and suffering. Do the Indians in the novel view poverty as natural or inevitable? On the other hand, as an outsider, does Kenny have a superior moral view of his own poverty that contradicts his obligation to vanquish it for others?

Chew on Poverty

Poverty limits the characters financially, but it is not ultimately a totally confining force, and is perhaps even an elevating one. As the characters have no material goods, they're forced to seek greater meaning in philosophical and spiritual happiness.

Poverty is an utterly despicable force that is powerful in the book because it is dealt with so honestly. Rukmani never romanticizes her poverty, instead speaking openly of hunger, hurt pride, and suffering. Her tale takes the mystery out of the anonymous destitute we imagine in homeless shelters and refugee camps. This story is not one of hope, but a challenge to the reader to do something about the arbitrary cruelty of poverty.

Theme of The Home

The home is a place of stability in this novel. The home represents safety and protection, but it is also the keeper of people's larger lives. When Rukmani packs up her home to go, she leaves it only physically. Her home lives on in her memory, and it travels with her as she struggles to pray. Ultimately, Nathan and Rukmani dream of returning to their home, and to the memory of the life they once had. Their home is not a place that exists any longer, but it's a space in memories and emotions that symbolizes their sense of belonging. When Nathan and Rukmani's sons leave home, they are leaving behind their whole lives. Selvam and Ira, who chose to stay in their village and take back their mother, represent the hope of stability and love. They have become a spiritual home, which is a familiar comfort for a dying old woman.

Questions About The Home

1. When Rukmani first sees the home Nathan built for her, she nearly cries out in despair. Compare this scene to her reaction when she is forced to leave her modest home at the end of part one of the novel. Is her life proof that one can be worn down to get used to anything, or does her home become something greater than a dwelling because of memory and experience?
2. Do Arjun and Thambi really think they'll ever return home? How does Ruku know they won't? Is the home a safe and comforting space or a confining one? How do the different generations of Ruku's family view the home differently?
3. Rukmani and Nathan romanticize their village home once they're away from it. Is this the

foolishness of the "grass is always greener" way of thinking, or have they really realized the value of their hometown, in spite of the financial destitution they know they'll find there? In the second part of the novel, what is it about their home that Nathan and Rukmani come to value?

4. One could argue that the family home belongs to Ira first – she's the first one that is actually born into it. When she is sent back from her husband's house, she returns to the fold of her family in spite of the shame brought by her albino child born of prostitution. Is Ira really welcome back into her home? Does Rukmani's treatment of her change, and what does this tell us about Ira's place in the home?

Chew on The Home

Nathan's home is the land, while Rukmani's home is wherever her husband is. Arjun and Thambi could not be at home without financial assurance, and Ira's home is where she can be accepted with her child. Different characters locate their home differently, as home is not a physical location but a state of mind dictated by comfort.

Home is equally a space of comfort and confinement, depending on whose perspective you're considering. For example, the only way Kenny can be comfortable is by having no single place of comfort. He is at home in his own displacement.

Theme of Love

Nectar in a Sieve is full of all different kinds of love. Family love, romantic love, love for children, and abstract philosophical love of life and land, are all central to the novel. The ability to endure throughout hardship is one of the most present motifs in the book, and often takes the form of love. Rukmani fears she cannot go on without her love, and when she comes back to her home, she has made peace with herself, likely inspired and comforted by her love for Puli and her children. An interesting note on family love – it's not a guarantee that love and understanding follow from being related or married in this novel – a lot of the novel is about the genesis of love between people. Nathan and Ruku come to know each other, and Ruku comes to know Puli in a way that shows love is about the growth of relationships.

Questions About Love

1. What role does love play in arranged marriages? Is the custom of arranged marriages accepted without questioning in the book? Do Ruku and Nathan love each other because they kind of have to?
2. Does Ruku ever express things that make us certain she *loves* her children? There's never an explicit "I love you" moment in the book, though we do see acts of endearment and sacrifice. Does Ruku's relationship to her children seem to be based on love, or rather on an understanding of mutual familial obligations?
3. How might one describe the relationship between Ruku and Kenny? Though there is never sexual indiscretion, the two do share a kind of intimacy that even Ruku sometimes finds surprising. Is the relationship between Ruku and Kenny a totally appropriate one? Why or why not?

4. Why does Ruku come to rely on Puli, in the city and in the village in her later life? Why does she assert that he's her adopted child? Does Ruku love Puli, and if so, what makes her love him? Is it a two-way thing?

Chew on Love

Selvam is the only one in the family who loves Sacrabani immediately and without reservation. Ira cries a lot, and Ruku and Nathan still have their doubts about the odd child. Ultimately, Selvam, who has sacrificed so much for the family and saves them all in the end, is the only character who understands the true meaning of unconditional family love.

Love is one of the most subtle and powerful, forces in the book. It isn't spoken of explicitly, but it imbues nearly every choice made by the characters we meet. Its quiet presence makes it more powerful than a more concrete force.

Theme of Foreignness and 'The Other'

Foreignness is most present in this novel as a trope of colonialism. The colonial world has brought in unfamiliar objects, people, and ways of life. The tannery, the Muslims that come to work at the tannery, the white men, the caste-breaking, and the breakdown social structure are all changes that intrude on people's lives, and are difficult to bear because they are so alien to what is normal. The colonial world is to blame for bringing strange and foreign things, and for disrupting traditions, but there's also other foreignness central to the novel. Characters are often foreign to each other. Ruku's children make decisions she doesn't understand, and she can't relate to Kunthi's love of the urban or Kenny's worldview about suffering. Foreignness is an inevitable part of relationships, and characters must learn to overcome it, by overlooking it, or, in better cases, by understanding it in order to communicate.

Questions About Foreignness and 'The Other'

1. Rukmani is foreign to Kenny in nearly every way, yet they forge a special relationship. How does foreignness operate in their interaction? Do they ever understand each other?
2. What types of foreignness exists in this novel, and how, if at all, can it be overcome? Is foreignness an obstacle, or an opportunity for learning and exchange?
3. Rukmani decides it is her wifely duty to essentially be subsumed by Nathan. But does she remain foreign or separate from him in any way?
4. Rukmani often feels foreign to her children, though they are her own flesh and blood. She often doesn't understand their actions. Does she try to make sense of the choices they make? Address especially her relationship and interactions with Selvam.

Chew on Foreignness and 'The Other'

Familiarity is not necessarily a central part of empathy; often it is those characters who are most foreign, who inspire the most sympathy. As ironic as it may seem, empathy may cause

characters in the novel to be less inclined to help each other. Because Rukmani is familiar with the problems that Janaki, Old Granny, and others in her community face, she is uninspired to help them, thinking they, should deal with their problems on their own. Had their woes been foreign to her, she might work harder to understand and help them.

Theme of Women and Femininity

Nectar in a Sieve hints at the fact that women did not have as much power in their society as men. The women of this novel, however, exercise tremendous and unusual power in many different ways. Rukmani is educated and savvy; her brave actions to seek fertility treatment allows her and Nathan to have sons, and even though she's technically subservient to Nathan, she's gained power in their relationship by gaining his love. Also, Rukmani exercises power by narrating her own story: she is in control of what we know, and has power over her readers. Ira and Kunthi turn to prostitution to gain economic power. This choice hints at the deeper power that women's sexuality gives them over men. Men may "own" them for a few minutes, but ultimately it's their allure that gives them power over men. Men have no choice but to seek their services, as the need they inspire is so great. Women are definitely restricted in a formal sense, but the women in this novel are constantly breaking and ignoring those restrictions – Ira raises her baby, Rukmani writes letters in the market place, Kenny's woman friend is a doctor – and while they all certainly *know* that they are women, this isn't the sole defining limitation on who they are or can be.

Questions About Women and Femininity

1. Is a shared femininity grounds for Rukmani to feel a sense of community with other women in the book? Does she seem closer to them, because they are women, than she does to her husband or sons?
2. How does Rukmani's attitude towards Ira change throughout the novel? In what ways do Rukmani and Ira represent the different opportunities women have, and different choices they make? Does Rukmani judge Ira? Does she ever empathize with Ira's plight as a woman? How does Rukmani's status as a daughter, mother, and wife inform her relationship with Ira?
3. What aspects of a woman's life define her within the novel? Are women considered solely for their roles with respect to men (as wives, daughters, and mothers) or are there independent aspects of their person that make them fully-fleshed out creatures?
4. Does the book capture the changing roles of women as India changes in the 20th century? What opportunities do the women have? Do they face prejudice or limitations as a result of their femininity? Is femininity within the novel political and historical, or is it rife with the universal problems women faced in a sexist society?

Chew on Women and Femininity

Women in the novel are guilty of judging each other in the same manner as they judged are by men. Rukmani especially accepts the limited and confining social roles women are supposed to play; this leads to a lack of empathy and empowerment among the women.

Women are allowed to be keepers of the home, which in this novel is a special source of power. Rukmani is no less powerful than Nathan, she just has a different sphere of influence than he does. This is supported by the fact that Nathan relies on Rukmani as an equal partner, not a subservient wife.

Theme of Power

Power is another important force in *Nectar in a Sieve*. Much of the novel is driven by the fact that the characters are often powerless against external circumstances. They are at the whim of the weather, the tannery, the landowners, and any other number of more powerful forces. However, power is also about the will of an individual. Though Rukmani and Nathan are forced into certain directions by outside power, those forces allow them to develop tremendous personal power. Nathan is buoyed by his convictions, and Rukmani has astonishing endurance and patience. The couple, though limited by external circumstance, has found that they need internal willpower in order to go on. In the landscape of the greater world, but the strength and bravery with which they face that outside world is a testament to their own personal power. They have hope in spite of everything around them, and this hope gives them the power to go on.

Questions About Power

1. When Rukmani says white men have power (9.31), what kind of power is she talking about? Is there any hint that Rukmani, or any of the other characters, resent the racial power structure in Indian society of the time? Is racial power understood differently between different classes of people? Different generations? Is the injustice of racial power ever explored in the book?
2. How do women have power in the book? Think about this with respect to the power of sexuality, power in the home, and power in larger society. How do different women in the book exercise their respective powers?
3. Nathan has powerful as the man of the house, but he is powerless when the tannery decides to buy up his land. How do hierarchies of power operate within the novel? What other hierarchies, besides those of economics, exist in the novel?
4. As Nathan and Rukmani age, power shifts from the old taking care of the young to the young taking care of the old. How do Nathan and Rukmani respond to this shift? Is there a sense that their children wield this power (and responsibility) with the same care and reverence that their parents did?

Chew on Power

The tannery is a powerful force in the village, and is has power over the opportunities and economic mobility of the characters. When the tannery officials come to seek Ruku's acceptance of their claim that they are not liable for Raja's death, they are implicitly admitting that they only hold power so long as the people allow them to hold power. This is symbolic of the larger hold of power that Britain and industry had over India – power can only be held unconditionally so long as it is not resisted or questioned.

It is only when characters put aside their considerations of their power relative to each other that

genuine loving and kindness can occur (as when Nathan eschews his power as a controlling husband, or Kenny overlooks his higher social position to befriend Ruku's family).

Life, Consciousness, and Existence Quotes

While the sun shines on you and the fields are green and beautiful to the eye, and your husband sees beauty in you which no one has seen before, and you have a good store of grain laid away for hard times, a roof over you and a sweet stirring in your body, what more can a woman ask for? (1.39)

Thought: Here Rukmani describes her ideal life. She delights in simple pleasures, and her ranking of important things includes food to eat and the beauty of the land. A happy life is made up of countless external factors, and while Rukmani is grateful for many of them, she can endure with only a few if she must.

"You chatter like a pair of monkeys," said Kali's husband, "with less sense. What use to talk of 'exchange' and so forth? Their life is theirs and yours is yours; neither change nor exchange is possible." (8.14)

Thought: Kali's husband thinks that there's no use in reflecting on and examining one's life, especially not relative to other people's. It's interesting that while Ruku is usually on the side of passively accepting what life brings to her, she can still judge the lives of others. She pities the Muslim women locked up at home. Though she doesn't understand them, they are actually in parallel situations, each having equally pitiable external circumstances over which they have no control.

"Whatever will they say?" I said, my face burning as he let me down again. "At our age too! You ought to be ashamed!"

"That I am not," he said, winking, to the vast delight of the onlookers. "I am happy because life is good and the children are good, and you are the best of all."

What more could I say after that? (10.17)

Thought: Nathan, like Ruku, sees life simply. He and his family are in the most joyous part of their lives, celebrating Deepavali together, and Nathan is overcome with emotion. His happiness doesn't rely on material goods, but rather he sees life as the sum of a good family and a good wife above all. It makes sense, then, that even in darkest times, Nathan can be incredibly happy and loving with his wife. She is probably the most central part of his life.

"Why fear?" said the old lady. "Am I note alone, and do I not manage?"

I thought of her sitting in the street all day long with the gunny sacking in front of her piled with a few annas' worth of nuts and vegetables; and I thought of Ira doing the same thing, and I was silent.

"It is not unbearable," said she, watching me with her shrewd eyes. "One gets used to it.:

It is true, one gets used to anything. I had got used to the noise and the smell of the tannery; they no longer affected me. I had seen the slow, calm beauty of our village wilt in the blast from town, and I grieved no more; so now I accepted the future and Ira's lot in it;... (11.47)

Thought: Faced with Old Granny's poverty and isolation, Ruku has to admit that life is inescapably hard, especially for lone women. However, Old Granny offers the view that life is about adaptability and the ability to get used to anything. Ruku relinquishes her worry a little bit about this: one cannot strive in the face something against which one is powerless. Life is about change, and no amount of worrying will change that.

What was it we had to learn? To fight against tremendous odds? What was the use? One only lost the little one had. Of what use to fight when the conclusion is known? (12.23)

Thought: Rukmani disagrees with the assertion of Kenny and her sons that people must learn to fight for what they want. Ruku is not a risk-taker. To her, the potential consequences must out-weigh the potential risks. It's important here to note that it isn't that Ruku doesn't *understand* that one can fight. Rather, she has thought about it and still decides that fighting isn't worth it. In this passage, she proves she isn't just a mindless pushover – instead she sees her life as a balance of the desired and the possible.

"Would you have us wasting our youth chafing against things we cannot change?" (12.51)

Thought: Ruku's sons are very different than her and Nathan. Arjun responds sharply to her that the idea of wasting away one's youth working against impossible odds is foolish. Of course, this is similar to what Ruku and Nathan have done, sticking their heads in the sand when life seems to offer them no options. The difference is not that they are less ambitious than their sons, but perhaps that they are less angry, and more accepting. Nathan and Ruku decided long ago that it is easier to stay and bear poverty in a place they know, than to set off to ills they know not of elsewhere. Even if it's a poor life, this is their life.

"Let us not sacrifice the future to our immediate need."

"What is the alternative?" he shouted. "Do you think I am blind and do not see, or so stupid as to believe that crops are raised without seed? Do you take me for a fool that—"

He was not shouting at me, but at the terrible choice forced upon us; (13.57)

Thought: This is only one of the many such choices that Ruku and Nathan have to make – faced with the problem of alleviating immediate poverty, they are essentially forced to cut off their hands to pay for their feet. Whether they're selling their seed for the land or collecting dung off the land to fuel their stoves instead of letting it be fertilizer, they're constantly sacrificing the present for the future.

Hope, and fear. Twin forces that tugged at us first in one direction, and then another, and which was the stronger no one could say. Of the latter, we never spoke, but it was always with us. Fear, constant companion of the peasant. (14.3)

Thought: Rukmani accepts that fear rules her life. Hope is a salve, but fear is the far more overpowering of the two. Ultimately, it feels like hope is the kind of thing one tells oneself in worst moments, a gentle lie to stave off the impending darkness.

Privately I thought, Well, and what if we gave in to our troubles at every step! We would be pitiable creatures indeed to be so weak, for is not a man's spirit given to him to rise above his misfortunes? As for our wants, they are many and unfilled, for who is so rich or compassionate as to supply them? Want is our companion from birth to death, familiar as the seasons or the earth, varying only in degree. What profit to bewail that which has always been and cannot change? (19.36)

Thought: Rukmani vacillates between viewing her acceptance of the world as a strength and as a weakness. She has a noble spirit, choosing to endure in the face of adversity. On the other hand, her nobility is the necessary consequence of her life. Maybe she could give in to the hopelessness around her, but what would that accomplish? In the end, perhaps what seems like nobility isn't that at all – just the necessary lens, a lie one tells oneself.

So it had been with my sons, so it was now with Old Granny, one day it might be the same for me, for all of us. A man might drift to his death before his time unnoticed, but when he was dead and beyond any care then at last he was sure of attention… (21.3)

Thought: Death is indeed an expected end to life. But it may also be a welcome reprieve. The meticulous care a deceased person is painful to Rukmani because it sharply contrasts the fact that such care is missing in life. It's as if the care people wish they could give to each other is reserved for one big farewell, once a person is no longer there to make demands.

Suffering Quotes

"At least it stood until the worst was over," said Kali to me, "and by God's grace we were all spared." She looked worn out; in the many years I had known her I had never seen her so deflated. She had come to ask for some palm leaves to thatch the new hut her husband was building; but I could only point to the blackened tree, its head bitten off and hanging by a few fibres from the withered stump.

"We must thatch our roof before the night," I said. "The rains may come again. We need rice too." (7.12)

Thought: Usually, suffering inspires empathy and sympathy from others. In this situation, though, everyone is suffering, and it seems no one has anything to share or give each other. Ruku deals with this delicate situation in a rather matter-of-fact way by denying help to her friend. It might seem a little harsh to us, but in desperate times, everyone's pretty much on his own. It's a bit jarring, and it makes us think that when Ruku's family falls on hard times, no one will be there to help them. Still, Ruku expects to be treated that way, so maybe it's not a big deal when she treats others that way.

"Times are better, times are better," he shouts. "Times will not be better for many months. Meanwhile you will suffer and die, you meek, suffering fools. Why do you keep this ghastly silence? Why do you not demand—cry out for help—do something?" (7.44)

Thought: For Kenny, the solution to suffering is to cry out. He thinks the people don't cry out because they somehow think the suffering is noble. What he does not realize is that sometimes when you cry out, there's no one there to help or listen. To Kenny, something must be done about suffering. To Ruku, it's all well and good that something *should* be done, but that doesn't mean anything *will,* be done. She reasons that it is best to grin and bear one's burden, rather than be disappointed when no help arrives.

How heartless are the young! One would have thought from his words we had purposefully starved him, when in fact of what there was he always got the biggest share after my husband.

"So," I said, "we do not do enough for you. These are fine words from an eldest son. They do not make good hearing."

"You do everything you can," he said. "It is not enough. I am tired of hunger and I am tired of seeing my brothers hungry. There is never enough, especially since Ira came to live with us." (9.22)

Thought: Rukmani knows that she's been trying her best, and that her best is not enough. Still, she resents this fact being pointed out. To her, suffering is an opportunity for everyone to put their lot in together, and really get through it as a group. Arjun has less romantic notions about suffering – he's hungry, and while his mom might get an "A" for effort, that's not filling his empty belly. He, like Kenny, thinks there are ways to get around suffering instead of accepting it nobly.

Nathan said not a word. There was a crushed look about him which spoke of the deep hurt he had suffered more than any words could have done. He had always wanted to own his own land, through the years there had been the hope, growing fainter with each year, each child, that one day he would be able to call a small portion of land his own. Now even his sons knew it

would never be. (9.37)

Thought: Suffering in this book is bigger than the small failures of crops and harvests. Nathan's whole life is wrapped up in the land. When his sons cruelly point out that they won't work on the land because the land will never be theirs, they aren't just getting out of fieldwork. They're crushing their father's spirit. Suffering doesn't only come from droughts and monsoons – sometimes it's the people closest to you that can hurt you the most.

"Enough!" he shouted. "More than enough has been said. Our children must act as they choose to, not for our benefit. Is it not enough that they suffer?"

The veins on his forehead were bulging. I had never seen him so angry before. Kali went away. Then the men went too, father and sons, leaving me alone who had no understanding. (12.30)

Thought: In *Nectar in a Sieve*, father and sons suffer in different ways. Ruku doesn't grasp any of it, perhaps because it is the quietly desperate suffering of men who cannot provide for their family. Because this burden does not belong to Ruku, she cannot understand this problem. Nathan likely feels impotent because he cannot provide for his family. Still, the desertion of his sons only adds to his suffering and his wounded pride. He must now go at it alone, and they have robbed him of both physical help and morale.

"That is why he and his kind are employed," Nathan said bitterly. "To protect overlords from such unpleasant tasks. Now the landlord can wring from us his moneys and care not for the misery he evokes, for indeed it would be difficult for any man to see another starve and his wife and children as well; or to enjoy the profits born of such travail." (13.23)

Thought: It seems that suffering only exists in the world because people who are not suffering can close their eyes to it. It would be hard to eat your dinner while watching one of those "Save the Children" commercials, but it is pretty easy to change the channel. Sivaji the Collector is essentially the means for the Zemindar to not have to see the suffering he causes others.

There we were, the four of us, hysterical, released, rocking with laughter and gasping for breath which ran out as fast as we sucked it in. The hollow cheeks and bulging stomachs, the grotesque, jutting bones, became matter for laughter; already, though they were still with us, in our minds they belonged to the past—to the painful past that we thrust from us with all our force; and the laughter was in some measure born of relief that we could do so. (17.2)

Thought: At some point, the degree to which this family suffers is actually absurd. It seems like there is always something devastating occurring: starvation, losing daughters to prostitution, monsoons, drought, etc. The characters of this story seem to only be able to make sense of it through laughter. Their laughter is strange: in some ways it's triumphant, but in other ways, it's really just an opportunity to recognize the utter insanity and great irony of everything that's happened to them. Laughter takes power and gravity away from suffering, but it also might be the only way one can react to a suffering that is inexplicable and unjustifiable.

Nevertheless, after a little while he did go to her and his gentleness melted her last remnants of control, for she began to weep. I heard her crying for a long time. (22.30)

Thought: Ruku is at first alarmed that Ira shows no signs of horror or revulsion at her own child. When Ira finally does break down, Rukmani doesn't go to her. Is this Ruku breathing a sigh of relief that her daughter is not crazy? Does Ruku feel ashamed at all for not alleviating any of Ira's suffering?

For all their play they looked as if they had never eaten a full meal in their lives, with their ribs thrusting out and bellies full-blown like drums with wind and emptiness; and they were also extremely dirty with the dust of the roadside and the filth deposited upon it; and the running sores many of them had upon their bodies were clogged with mud where blood or pus had exuded. But they themselves were forgetful of their pains—or patient with tem as the bullock had been—and played naked and merry in the sun. (25.16)

Thought: Suffering isn't the only emotion present in the novel. Even in the most awful situations, there are moments of joy to be snatched from the clutches of despair. These street kids have the same desire for joy that other kids do, even if they don't live totally normal lives and are reduced to scrapping over crusts.

There is no touching this girl, I thought. Misfortune has hardened her, which is just as well, she will take many a knock yet. (26.50)

Thought: Ammu's approach to suffering is essentially the exact opposite of Ruku's. While Ruku bears her suffering with piety and an obstinate hopefulness, Ammu has decided to view the world as one big place full of people trying to take advantage of her. Still, you might not be able to blame the girl for being so harsh – Ruku always has Nathan to share the burden, while Ammu suffers alone.

Transformation Quotes

How quickly children grow! They are infants—you look away a minute and in that time they have left their babyhood behind. Our little girl ran about in the sun bare and beautiful as she grew, with no clothes to hamper her limbs or confine her movements. Then one day when she was five—long before Arjun was born—Nathan pointed her out to me as she played in the fields.

"Cover her," he said. "It is time."

I wanted to cry out that she was a baby still, but of course Nathan was right; she had left infancy forever. (3.38)

Thought: From the moment that Ira stops being an infant, she is burdened with what it means to be a woman in this society. Her life will change: her parents will clothe her, and the restrictions on her behavior and movement will increase until she's finally sent off to be married. Though her parents make these changes and restrictions against her with the best of intentions, nothing will protect her from the world.

Change I had known before, and it had been gradual. My father had been a headman once, a person of consequence in our village: I had lived to see him relinquish this importance, but the alteration was so slow that we hardly knew when it came. I had seen both my parents sink into old age and death, and here too there was no violence. But the change that now came into my life, into all our lives, blasting its way into our village, seemed wrought in the twinkling of an eye. (4.1)

Thought: Ruku has a million reasons to resent the tannery, but she suggests that it's the swiftness of the transformation it brought about that's hardest to bear. It's not just the tannery itself that bothers Ruku. What upsets Rukmani most is the fact that even from its earliest building stages, it was clear that the tannery would change the pace of village life. It's almost as if the changes brought about by the tannery bleed into nearly every facet of Ruku's life.

"Besides, you will not want me so often," I said. "This home, your brothers, are all you have known so far, but when you have your own home and your own children you will not miss these… (6.8)

Thought: A woman traditionally leaves her father's house for her husband's house. Rukmani knows that Ira will miss her, but she seems pretty comfortable with Ira essentially trading her old family for a new family. Rukmani can be wistful about this, but the reality is that her daughter's success will require cutting ties with her past and setting up shop elsewhere. Rukmani seems to accept this change glibly, as she does with most things that pain her deeply.

Then as happens even in the brightest moment, I remembered Janaki. Last year she had come with us, she and her children. This year who knew—or cared? The black thought momentarily doused the glow within me; then, angered and indignant, I thrust the intruder away, chasing it, banishing it… tired of gloom, reaching desperately for perfection of delight, which can surely never be. (10.5)

Thought: Rukmani can't afford to think of the fates of the people whose lives are changing around her. She's just on the cusp of great disaster herself, and if she thinks of Janaki she'll be forced to remember the instability and uncertainty they all share, relying on the land. Pushing away thoughts of Janaki is Rukmani's futile attempt to pretend the current happiness and stability she's having are going to last.

"I will have an answer."

"I can give you none."

Nathan's brows drew together: she had never before spoken to him in this manner. Looking at her, it seemed to me that almost overnight she had changed; she had been tender and modest and obedient, now she had relinquished every one of these qualities; it was difficult to believe she had ever been their possessor. (16.52)

Thought: Before she turned to some way to make a little money, Ira was just moping around the house, ashamed of her barrenness. Her change of attitude is actually pretty understandable. In the face of the other changes she experienced, such as losing her husband, Ira was a passive victim. With this change of career, Ira is actually making her own choice: she's transformed from a victim to an agent of her own fate. It's kind of empowering, even though her choice leads to an illegal activity.

Not in the town, where all that was natural had long been sacrificed, but on its outskirts, one could still see the passing of the season. For in the town there were the crowds, and streets battened down upon the earth, and the filth that men had put upon it; and one walked with care for what might lie beneath one's feet or threaten from before or behind; and in this preoccupation forgot to look at the sun or the stars, or even to observe they had changed their setting in the sky: and knew nothing of the passage of time save in dry frenzy, by looking at a clock. But for us, who lived by the green, quiet fields, perilously close though these were to the town, nature still gave its muted message. Each passing day, each week, each month, left its sign, clear and unmistakable. (20.1)

Thought: The center of the town changes dramatically, but the outskirts remain village-like. The transformation of the seasons is still visible in the village areas – though the people of the town can't afford to notice it. The seasons will continue to happen reliably, whether or not people recognize them any longer.

He understood her well, better than I did who was her mother; in fact, I wonder whether parents ever know their children as they know one another. (22.1)

Thought: Ruku's children are her joy and pride – indeed she wasn't a happy woman until she had sons. The fact that Ruku begins to recognize the closeness her children share with each other signals a change in her own thinking. Her children do not really belong to her. Ruku resigns herself to the fact that they'll do what they want, and that she'll never be able to rely on knowing who they are. Ruku's realization helps her deal with her children as they evolve from obedient boys and girls to independent, and sometimes rebellious, men and women (i.e. when Selvam chooses to leave the land, and Ira turns to selling her body).

"What can we do? There are many like ourselves who cannot provide for the future. You know it yourself."

"Yes; I know…. I do not know why I asked; it was needless. There is no provision at all," he said, speaking half to himself, "neither for old nor young nor sick. They accept it; they have no option." (23.22)

Thought: This is the first time Kenny admits that Ruku has a point. He seems a bit worn down by the desperation, suffering, and uncertainty around him. He's finally able to admit that maybe people around him are in insurmountably difficult situations. It's interesting that he doesn't sound broken, just realistically resigned to reality.

There had been a time when we, too, had benefited—those days seemed very remote now, almost belonging to another life—but we had lost more than we had gained or could ever regain. Ira had ruined herself at the hands of the throngs that the tannery attracted. None but these would have laid hands on her, even at her bidding. My sons had left because it frowned on them; one of them had been destroyed by its ruthlessness. And there were others its touch had scathed. Janaki and her family, the hapless chakkli Kannan, Kunthi even…. (23.57)

Thought: Ruku looks at the tannery as a major force of negative change in her life. It's notable that she has all of this angry feeling towards the tannery, but later she'll admit that nature has as much of an effect on her wellbeing as the tannery. She seems to be more accepting of nature's impact, whereas she really resents the tannery for its influence. We've got to wonder how this is justifiable in her mind, when they are both just external circumstances over which she has little control.

As it was we said no more—not that night at any rate, although subsequently we had more discussions than I can recount—accepting only that we were to go and that our children and grandchild were to stay. (23.94)

Thought: This is a major change in roles of the family – the parents can no longer take care of the children, but the children cannot yet take care of the parents. There's pain in the separation, but it's also painful to think of how much Nathan and Ruku sacrificed for their children, only to come to this point. The land they've worked so hard for, in the end, is a thing they have to leave.

Man and the Natural World Quotes

Nature is like a wild animal that you have trained to work for you. So long as you are vigilant and walk warily with thought and care, so long will it give you its aid; but look away for an instant, be heedless or forgetful, and it has you by the throat. (7.1)

Thought: Ruku's thinking about nature might be a little naïve. Whether she's looking at Nature or not, it's going to do what it darn well pleases. Of course she and Nathan have little effect on the land (like, crops will grow where they plant seed) but ultimately nature has the final say.

"Words and words," said Kunthi. "Stupid words. No wonder they call us senseless peasant women; but I am not and never will be. There is no earth in my breeding."

"If there were you would be the better for it," said I wrathfully, "for then your values would be true." (8.1)

Thought: Nature is equated with moral goodness in Ruku's mind. For Kunthi, Nature's simplicity is reflective of a lack of urban sophistication. Each woman interprets nature differently. Where do these beliefs come from? This is akin to a chicken/egg situation: maybe they get their beliefs from their observations of nature, or maybe they selectively see in nature only what confirms their beliefs.

"Two more mouths to feed," she complained. "Only one of my three sons had the sense to go back. I do not know what is to become of us, for the land cannot sustain us all. So much for reading and writing," she said, accusing me with eye and finger. (12.25)

Thought: Kali blames Ruku for her own difficulties: she (Kali) complains that the land can't sustain her family. It is interesting to note that this would have been true whether or not Ruku had educated her kids. Kali is presenting a false dichotomy, as if the incompatibility of nature and learning is to blame her troubles. (It is actually the tannery, and its refusal to pay properly, that are at fault).

He coaxed me out into the sunlight and we sat down together on the brown earth that was part of us, and we gazed at the paddy fields spreading rich and green before us, and they were indeed beautiful. (12.63)

Thought: When Ruku and Nathan are disappointed by the external circumstances of their life, particularly their sons' choices, they turn to the land for spiritual healing. It is almost as though the land is as much a part of them as their own children.

I took the paddy from him and parted the grass and there within its protective husk lay the rice-grain, just big enough to see, white, perfect, and holding in itself our lives. (12.65)

Thought: Ruku and Nathan minister to the land and often talk of how they see it as a part of themselves, but here we get the hint that actually Nature is in control. The seeds metaphorically hold their lives, but the land is literally in control of their lives – if they do not harvest they do not eat.

...before long the rain came lashing down, making up in fury for the long drought and giving the grateful land as much as it could suck and more. But in us there was nothing left—no joy, no call for joy. It had come too late. (13.73)

Thought: Nature alone cannot provide happiness, even if it is forgiving after it has been so cruel.

The sowing of seed disciplines the body and the sprouting of the seed uplifts the spirit, but there is nothing to equal the rich satisfaction of a gathered harvest... (17.9)

Thought: Ruku is continually hurt by the drought as it slowly kills her loved ones. Here we see her tactic for endurance: she constantly rationalizes, as though her interaction with the land is part of her own personal development. This kind of rationalization may be dangerous, but it is perhaps the only way Ruku can survive against these terrible odds. The rich harvest is not a given consequence of discipline and an uplifted spirit, it's just a joyous coincidence that has more to do with luck than with anything else.

This is one of the truths of our existence as those who live by the land know: that sometimes we eat and sometimes we starve. We live by our labours from one harvest to the next, there is no certain telling whether we shall be able to feed ourselves and our children, and if bad times are prolonged we know we must see the weak surrender their lives and this fact, too, is within our experience. In our lives there is no margin for misfortune. (23.58)

Thought: Ruku recognizes that the yield of the land is rather arbitrary – sometimes it delivers and sometimes it doesn't. When she's frank like this with us, it puts the rest of her philosophical talk about the religious value of suffering and endurance in perspective. It's as though she knows, deep down, that this isn't about a moral or philosophical life, but about simply feeding one's family. The moral and philosophical stuff is just a way to deal with the arbitrarily cruel forces of nature, almost a self-delusional pacification, and Ruku seems to concede that here.

With each passing day the longing for the land grew; our plans were forged against a background of brown earth and green fields and the ripe rustling paddy, not, curiously, as they were, but as we had first known them... fresh, open and unspoilt, with their delicate scents and sounds untainted, with skies clear above them and the birds finding sanctuary in the grasses. And at the same time, keeping pace with these longings, our distaste for the city grew and grew and became a sweeping, pervading hatred. (27.9)

Thought: Ruku and Nathan's remoteness from their land has allowed them to romanticize it – they think of it fondly because they only remember the good times there, not the bad times that drove them to the city in the first place. They're basically suffering from emotional and economic dislocation, and they use their dislocation from the land as a proxy for their frustrations. They well know that Nature is not a magically happy place, and returning to it will not solve anything, but while they're away from it, they can dream of it being better than it actually was, because it's definitely better than where they are now. (Or is it?).

I remember looking up for the flare that had ever burnt on the top of the temple, and it was quenched; and the black demons of fear came shrieking at my ear and would not be silenced, for all that I repeated like a madwoman, "Fire cannot burn in water." (29.2)

Thought: Ruku knows Nathan is dying. Of all the things she's endured in her life, this one alone cannot be rationalized. We see if she hadn't been doing that the whole time, she might have been driven to madness. It brings to mind Hamlet's potent line to Horatio in Shakespeare's *Hamlet*, "There are more things in heaven and earth, Horatio, Than are dreamt of in your philosophy." (For more on *Hamlet*, see our module.) Ruku could bear the cruelty of nature to her harvests and livelihood, but she cannot bear nature's inevitable touch of death. Like her other philosophical moments, she's philosophizing on the truth of nature, but this philosophy doesn't bring her any comfort – it only exposes that man is powerless in the face of natural events.

Poverty Quotes

To the children I handed out two annas apiece, to be spent on fireworks. I had never been able to do so before -- in previous years we had contented ourselves with watching other people's fireworks, or with going down to the bonfire in the village, and even now I felt qualms about wasting money on such quickly spent pleasures; but their rapturous faces overcame my misgivings. It is only once, I thought, a memory. (10.1.)

Thought: Ruku is usually very frugal, so her decision to spend on a little extravagance is quite meaningful. It's a reminder of what it really means to be in poverty, and it helps the reader to see the characters as more than archetypes of people living in dire poverty, anonymous faces crowded together in food lines at refugee camps. Poverty is about worrying how you'll provide simple necessities for your family. This is why things that are small, like fireworks or the dum-dum cart, are so meaningful. Though they seem like nothing, they come at great costs.

"What is it that calls you?" I said. "Is it gold? Although we have none, remember that money isn't everything."

"It is an important part of living," he answered me patiently, "and work is another. There is nothing for us here, for we have neither the means to buy land nor to rent it." (12.50)

Thought: Ruku has resigned herself to living in poverty, and she says it's because she's come around to realizing that money isn't everything. From her narrative, we know she enjoys living on the land, and she gets her pleasure from it. Her sons, by contrast, show no such proclivity for the land. Because they do they not share her pleasure in the land, they don't share her comfort with the consequent poverty of living on the land.

At one time there had been kingfishers here, flashing between the young shoots for our fish; and paddy birds; and sometimes, in the shallower reaches of the river, flamingoes, striding with ungainly precision among the water reeds, with plumage of a glory not of this earth. Now birds came no more, for the tannery lay close—except crows and kites and such scavenging birds, eager for the town's offal… (12.63)

Thought: Poverty is bigger than just economic poverty. The novel mainly focuses on the financial troubles of Ruku's family caused by the tannery, but the tannery's impact is even greater. The land has been robbed and become poverty-stricken by the tannery's actions. The birds are gone, the water is polluted, a stench pervades the town – ultimately the landscape suffers as irrevocably as the people.

She had no relatives left—no person on whom she had any claim—certainly there was no one to enquire whether she made a living or how much longer she could continue to do so. Better to avoid such questions, better to pass quickly by with a cheerful word than to stop and ask, for who would lightly take on the burden of feeding another mouth? And so one day she quietly disappeared. They found her body on the path that led to the well, an empty mud pot beside her and the gunny sacking tied around her waist. She had died of starvation. (21.2)

Thought: Old Granny was alone in her poverty, and Ruku had to be remote from her because of Ruku's own poverty. Poverty not only makes you unable to help yourself, it puts you in a position where you can't help others, no matter how much you want to. Ruku lives in a community beset by poverty, and its crippling effect often incapacitates the community. It costs friendships and lives, and there is nothing to be done in the face of it. One can only walk by and pretend to ignore the hungry bellies of others, as if unable to hear over one's own rumbling stomach.

"I would do so if only it were in my hands. But what comfort can one offer a man who sees his family wholly dependent on him and no one else to see to them?" (23.7)

Thought: Ruku worries that she sounds selfish when she says Nathan has good reason to be worried because his whole family relies on him. Still, she knows it's the truth. The family lives in poverty, in some part, because of Nathan's choice to stay on rented land (and his inability to buy it). They rely entirely on Nathan to just get by. Ultimately there's little anyone else in the family can do to get them out of poverty, as Ruku says the land is a man's domain. As the other men in their life have deserted them, their poverty rests on Nathan's shoulders. The cultural and physical bounds of society (where only men can do valuable economic work on the land) are intertwined with the economic reality of poverty.

"We must go to Murugan. He has a good job—I am sure he will welcome his parents."

"It is a long way. With respect, you are not as young or as fit as you were."

"Yet the effort must be made," said Nathan, "for we cannot live except by the land, for I have no

other knowledge or skill; and as you say I am getting on and for me it would be impossible to find another landlord. Who indeed would rent his land to such as I am, past hard labour and uncertain of paying what I owe?" (23.71)

Thought: Poverty is crippling – you work and work to make just enough to get by, and in the end you sacrifice your future. Nathan has been able to keep his family afloat with the work of his body – still, he has not made enough to protect them in the time when his body is broken. In the end, his only recourse is to beg for charity from his son. Work kept his family just shy of poverty, so once he is unable to work, his family ends up in dire straits. This isn't just a Third World problem of the past; it's the plight of the modern poor who don't make enough for retirement, and who can't pay their medical bills once they no longer work. Again, poverty is a feedback loop, you can't get out of it once you're in it, and there's no lifesaver but charity.

Merry, that is, until a crust of bread fell on the road or a sweetmeat toppled from an over-ambitious pyramid when, all childishness lost, all play forgotten, they fought ferociously in the dust for the food. (25.16)

Thought: Poverty has taken childhood away from these children – they're reduced to mere animals. In spite of the happiness they find in play, their poverty is ultimately a greater defining force in their lives.

"Outsiders should not be allowed," they grumbled. "Are there not enough destitute in this city without the whole of India flocking in?"

We looked at them resentfully: were we not as hungry as they? Soon we were looking at newcomers with a fearful eye, wondering with each fresh new arrival how much less there would be. (27.6)

Thought: We see in the novel how poverty breeds isolation, competitiveness, pettiness, and suffering. When Ruku has these simple fears when she looks at other poverty-stricken people, the problem suddenly becomes a lot clearer. There simply isn't enough to go around, and even what little people get from charity is only going to be diminished by the ever-expanding need for charity.

But how? We have no money. My husband can till and sow and reap with skill, but here there is no land. I can weave and spin, or plait matting, but there is no money for spindle, cotton or fibre. For where shall a man turn who has no money? Where can he go? Wide, wide world, but as narrow as the coins in your hand. Like a tethered goat, so far and no farther. Only money can make the rope stretch, only money. (27.11)

Thought: Here we see the vicious cycle of poverty – without a little money, it seems one can't make a little money. Poverty is a dead end; and it adds insult to injury that one can see the road to riches, but can't take the first step onto it.

Plans, everyone had plans. They were all built on money. Save enough to keep dry, save enough to cast one's chains, save enough to go away. (28.39)

Thought: Poverty often hinges on making enough to get by, but provides no buffer. For the people striving to make a living (literally just enough to live on) the only safety buffer they have is making plans about what they'll do when they magically make a little extra money. Of course, this money will never come (and Ruku tells us as much here), but it seems these delusional and optimistic plans are necessary to keep one going in the face of certain poverty. Nathan used to lie to himself about buying a little land, Ruku used to think of saving for Ira's second dowry; it's only when Ruku sees other people making plans that she has the objectivity to realize they're all only fooling themselves. Poverty is their lot, and planning for an optimistic future is their soothing lie.

The Home Quotes

A few days after our conversation the shop finally closed down. Nobody asked: "Where do you go from here?" They did not say, "What is to become of us?" We waited and one day they came to bid us farewell, carrying their possessions, with their children trailing behind, all but the eldest, whom the tannery had claimed. Then they were gone, and the shopkeepers were glad that there was less competition, and the worker who moved into their hut was pleased to have a roof over his head, and we remembered them for a while and then took up our lives again. (8.9)

Thought: In order to maintain her own home, Ruku cannot afford to worry about the homes of others. This is an important moment to recognize that the home is a self-contained unit. People don't compete like they do in the city, but each woman must fend for her home and her home alone.

My husband especially had been looking forward to the day when they would join him in working the land; but Thambi only shook his head. (9.35)

Thought: Nathan envisions his sons will continue on the tradition of their agricultural profession. Their rejection of the land is more than a career choice. When they walk away from the family land, they're walking away from their family and their place in the home. (Ironically, Nathan had wanted sons to work alongside him, and he endures and sacrifices to raise them, only to be deserted by them.)

They spoke soothingly—of how much they would earn, and how one day they would return—as one does to a child; and I listened to them; and it was all a sham, a poor shabby pretense to mask our tortured feelings.

They left at first daylight, each carrying a bundle with food in it, and each before he went kissed Nathan's feet, then mine, and we laid our hands on them in blessing. I knew we would never see them again. (12.56)

Thought: The eldest boys, who had almost specifically been bred to work alongside their father, and keep up the family tradition and home, are the first to leave. Ruku knows she'll never see them again, but she is silent about their desertion. Ironically, while boys were supposed to stay and keep the family, girls were meant to go off and become part of their husband's families. While Ruku slowly loses son after son to one thing or another, Ira is the one left behind (with Selvam) to hold together the family.

"I have the usual encumbrances that men have—wife, children, home—that would have put chains about me but I resisted, and so I am alone. As for coming and going, I do as I please, for am I not my own master?" (12.77)

Thought: Kenny, interestingly, will be echoed by Puli, who will later say he has no mother to worry over him or to worry him. With Kenny, there's always the tendency to interpret his words thinking about race or colonialism. When we think about what it means that Kenny and Puli share some of the same tendencies, we might recognize that both are just boys with wanderlust – they have no sense of home, maybe because they never could, or maybe because they didn't want it.

"We can do without these, but if the land is gone our livelihood is gone, and we must thenceforth wander like jackals." (13.25)

Thought: When the land actually *is* sold much later in the novel, Rukmani takes the time to reflect on all the memories she's had in her home. Nathan, by contrast, shows here that he's perhaps more practical and less romantic. Nathan's first concern is a roof and a livelihood – the home means a different thing to him than to Rukmani.

"…You live and work here, and there is in your heart solicitude for us and love for our children. But this is not your country and we are not your people. If you lived here your whole life it still would not be."

"My country," he said. "Sometimes I do not know which is my country. Until today I had thought perhaps it was this." (18.56)

Thought: The only thing that changed today was that Kenny actually arrived back in the village. It seems deep down, he has a tendency towards romantic optimism, as evidenced by his undying hope about building the hospital. Kenny likely thought of India as his home while he was away in his England because he didn't fit in there either. Kenny is perhaps too judgmental of every place to really comfortably fit in anywhere. He's at home in his own dislocation.

"I will not be a burden to you. I am happy enough here, people are used to me and to my son. I cannot start a new life now." (23.85)

Thought: Ira is at home in the village, even though it has been an unhappy place for her. Home is not always where one is joyful, but rather where one is comfortable. Ira has grown accustomed to hardship, and she'd rather face it at home than go seek it elsewhere. Ironically, her parents will also come to the same conclusion.

The promise of shelter had been kept however: food, and somewhere to sleep. (24.80)

Thought: The bundles contained the last remnants of Nathan and Ruku's old life. Losing them is a symbolic break with the old home. The new requirements for comfort are not as major as a place for family, security, and joy. Now, even basic accommodations, like food and shelter, are a comfort.

The children giggled delightedly, wriggling with pleasure. Their mother was peering into one of the pots on the fire, stirring and tasting. "Ready now," she said with satisfaction, wiping her streaming eyes with the corner of her sari. (25.74)

Thought: Markandaya subtly paints a picture in this paragraph. Rukmani is essentially observing an idyllic home, and you can bet she's imagining what it would be like to be sitting across from Ira, surrounded by her own grandchildren with a warm full pot on the stove. It's enough to comfort Ruku for the moment, but it's still a shining example of what Ruku and her family never will have.

"You had better go home," I said, nudging him. "What will your poor mother think if you stay here all night?"

"I have no mother, poor or otherwise," he said. "There is no one to worry about me and none to worry me either, which is a good thing," and turning on his side he fell instantly asleep. (27.54)

Thought: It's funny that after declaring he likes to be without an anchor in the world, Puli becomes attached to the old couple. Ruku's narration makes it seem like they depend on him more than he does on them. In the end, however, Puli returns to the village with Ruku. Though the boy is without an actual dwelling, he finds something of a home in the care and love of Rukmani and Nathan.

"You are too young to understand," said Nathan. "This is not my home, I can never live here." (27.125)

Thought: Nathan links his notion of home to his age. Strictly speaking, Nathan doesn't actually have a home to return to – no land belongs to him, and his hut is no longer a roof for his head. Home is metaphorical, more a memory from a past time than any certainty Nathan actually has to return to.

Love Quotes

My spirit ached with pity for her, I longed to be able to comfort her, to convince her that in a few months' time her new home would be the most significant part of her life, the rest only a preparation… (6.9)

Thought: On the one hand, Rukmani is giving away her first-born child, but on the other, she went through this same process of being given away. It's bittersweet that a mother must think on her own abandonment by her mother as she gives away her daughter. When a daughter does set up her new home, she will focus more on her new family than her old. We can't tell if Rukmani accepts this reality about "losing" the love and attention of her daughter because that's the way it is, or whether she's sad even though she knows Ira must go.

"I do not blame him," Nathan said. "He is justified, for a man needs children. He has been patient."

"Not patient enough," I said. "Not patient like you, beloved." (9.10)

Thought: Nathan shows himself to be a wonderful lover to Ruku. His observation here shows that he knows his "rights" as a man, or at least what he can deservedly expect out of a wife (namely children). But even as he admits that, it's still clear that he has sacrificed for Ruku, and to him it's been worth the wait. Ruku, too, acknowledges that she appreciates Nathan's patience and understanding. Their relationship is one of equal maturity, respect, and even adoration. Only this kind of loving devotion could sustain them in hard times.

Words died away, the listening air was very still, the black night waited. In the straining darkness I felt his body moving with desire, his hands on me were trembling, and I felt my senses opening like a flower to his urgency. I closed my eyes and waited, waited in the darkness while my being filled with a wild, ecstatic fluttering, waited for him to come to me. (10.21)

Thought: The passion that's in Ruku and Nathan's relationship is quite beautiful – they are more than economic and financial support for each other, they're real lovers.

As my pregnancy advanced she turned completely away from me. Sometimes I saw her looking at me with brooding, resentful eyes, and despite myself I cold not help wondering if hatred lay behind her glance. (11.39)

Thought: It seems like the reasonable thing for a loving mother to do would be to reach out to Ira. Though Ruku went so far as to bring Ira to Kenny for fertility treatment, it seems she treats Ira like a lost cause since her husband won't take her back. Perhaps Ira has hard feelings because she can feel that her life is essentially over. Ruku doesn't seem to do anything to dispel those feelings – it's a little surprising how little comfort and love she seems to give Ira in these hard days.

"It is as you say a long time ago," I said wearily. "That she is evil and powerful I know myself. Let it rest." (14.80)

Thought: Ruku and Nathan have already built their life together. They've known each other long enough that it's worth it to look over the indiscretions (Nathan's children with Kunthi, Ruku's visits to Kenny) if they want to sustain their marriage. Ironically, the relationship they've built is why they stay together, even though they've learned that relationship was built on some lies. Apparently the good parts of love are enough to get them through the bad parts. They're emotionally mature, but they're also really comfortable with each other.

"A baby is no worse for being conceived in an encounter."

"You may be right," I said bitterly, "but you do not realize the shame of it. People have not spared us." (18.69)

Thought: Rukmani has chosen to concern herself with the talk of others, instead of choosing to do right by her own daughter. She always knew Ira was meant to be a mother, and she knows what drove Ira to prostitution. Still, she cannot bring herself to be happy or supportive of her daughter. Again, her love of Ira seems compromised, perhaps because she values her own feelings above her love for Ira.

"I am not unaware," he said quietly. "But is it not sufficient that you have the strength and I have the trust?"

"It is indeed," I said with relief. "I wanted only that you should know."

We smiled at each other in perfect understanding. (19.17)

Thought: The love between Ruku and Selvam goes beyond that of mother and son. It's not just obedience or familial obligation that bonds them, but a real understanding of each other. This sheds some light on Selvam as a son, especially as he's different from his brothers. Ruku admits that she doesn't know him completely (like Ira does), but at least he sticks around. By contrast, her other sons, (whom she didn't know completely either) took this isolation from her as a good excuse to abandon the family. Selvam, though he has grown beyond the family, still stays with his parents out of love. The kind of understanding exhibited here is good proof that not just obligation, but real love, is what makes his relationship with Ruku work.

The woman is his, his wife, not only now for this surging experience, but tomorrow and next year. She will carry his seed and he will see her fruitful, watch while day by day his child grows within her. And so he is tender and careful, and comes to her clean that their fulfillment may be rich and blessed. (20.6)

Thought: Ruku worries that since Ira has no such love, her baby and her life are not going to be as blessed as what comes of a loving partnership. Ironically, she's thinking of her relationship with Nathan, even though she knows that Nathan has fathered two of Kunthi's children (which he obviously hasn't raised with the attention he's given his other children). Love is not a given for men, and even her own beloved man has fathered two children outside the bounds of love. Ruku doesn't think of this as she worries over Ira, but it's something to think about in the backdrop of these thoughts.

"Would you hold me when my time is come? I am at peace. Do not grieve." "If I grieve," I said "it is not for you, but for myself, beloved, for how shall I endure without you, who are my love and my life?" "You are not alone," he said "I live in my children." (29.9)

Thought: Ruku's love for Nathan is overwhelming. After most of their family has left them, and they've been forced to abandon their home, it's only reasonable that she should think of him as her only anchor in the world. Nathan's words here are a bit suspect. Of their seven children, three have disappeared, two are dead, and one has ruined her life as a prostitute. Nathan's comment should give us pause. We might wonder whether he only says it to comfort his wife (and doesn't believe it), or whether his love for his children and his family (in spite of everything that's happened) is still deep enough that he's willing to feel good that they are all he has as a legacy.

"My son," I said. "We adopted him, your father and I."

"You like tired and hungry," Ira said, taking his arm. "Come with me and rest, I will prepare the rice." (30.5)

Thought: Ira eases the situation of Puli's acceptance by being her usual loving self. That Ira takes him in immediately is another mark of her incredible emotional generosity (which is actually in stark contrast to her mother's attitude towards her). Ruku hesitated to accept Sacrabani, and even didn't want to sign on to taking care of Puli, but Ira will unhesitatingly love all children. Her gentle love promises to be an important part of holding the family together.

Foreignness and 'The Other' Quotes

"Why do you not demand—cry out for help—do something? There is nothing in this country, oh God there is nothing!" (7.44)

Thought: Kenny seems to think that one only needs to cry out for help in order to receive it. Rukmani, however, knows what it is to struggle for her and her own, and often believes that struggling against the inevitable is futile. Kenny's declaration that there is nothing in this country amounts to hopelessness; Ruku, by contrast, knows there is nothing in the country for people who are not willing to help themselves. Kenny, ever needing help and trying to help others, is engaged in a project that goes against the many values of his adopted country. His hopelessness is Ruku's reality. Even if he understands that, he still resents it.

"I waited all day," I gasped. "I must see you. My husband will be back soon and then I cannot come."

His frown deepened. He said coldly, "You people will never learn. It is pitiful to see your foolishness." (11.5)

Thought: Kenny judges Ruku's hesitation to be open with Nathan as "foolishness," and he ties that foolishness into her whole culture with "you people." Cultural sensitivity doesn't matter at all to him – in his eyes, whether this is about Indian culture or not, it's stupid. It's hard to tell whether Kenny's judgment of Indian culture implicitly assumes that he knows better, or comes from a superior culture.

"What has happened?" we ask with trepidation. They are still our sons, but suddenly they have outgrown us. (12.10)

Thought: Rukmani doesn't understand how the boys could agitate for more money, but it's interesting that she thinks of it as them having surpassed her and Nathan. She's basically the opposite of Kenny – her sons are doing something she doesn't understand, and she assumes it is because they are superior or have some greater understanding than she does, not because they're being foolish. Rukmani feels like she doesn't know the boys anymore, and she can't do anything about it. Her own children are adopting values that are foreign to her tradition, and so the boys have become foreign to her.

A strange nature, only partly within my understanding. A man half in shadow, half in light, defying knowledge. (12.83)

Thought: The relationship between Kenny and Rukmani is a strange one – Kenny seems to reveal things to Ruku that even he is surprised about. It's as if talking to her sometimes leads him to conclusions or realizations about himself. We get the sense that it's not just that Ruku doesn't understand Kenny; Kenny seems to actually be quite foreign to himself.

…Other farmers and their families, in like plight to ourselves, were also out searching for food; and for every edible plant or root there was a struggle—a desperate competition that made enemies of friends and put an end to humanity. (14.83)

Thought: The struggle against starvation has made people remote from their own humanity. Hunger has turned them into people they themselves don't even recognize, and it's also made them alien to each other. Their reliance on their natural surroundings has failed them and, ironically, has made them unnatural creatures, foreign to their natural selves.

"You simplify everything, being without understanding. Your views are so limited it is impossible to explain to you."

"Limited, yes," I agreed. "Yet not wholly without understanding. Our ways are not your ways."

"You have sound instincts," he said.

For the first time since I had known him I saw a spark of admiration in his eyes. (18.52)

Thought: Ruku reminds Kenny gently that they are not better or worse than each other, but they simply understand things differently. Her humble relativism checks his glib cultural superiority, and he knows it.

"Yet our priests fast, and inflict on themselves severe punishments, and we are taught to bear our sorrows in silence, and all this is so that the soul may be cleansed."

He struck his forehead. "My God!" he cried. "I do not understand you. I never will. Go before I am too entangled in your philosophies." (19.39)

Thought: There's a tension here: Kenny might not understand the foreign religious principles of Hinduism, or he might understand them and still disagrees with them. Here, we see that he avoids delving too deeply into the issue. Instead of exploring what Ruku believes and why, he'd rather dismiss her whole belief system as foreign. This is a glimpse of Kenny as convinced by his beliefs, and maybe lacking the interest, or the energy, to challenge them. He doesn't understand the ways of other people, but he has his own understanding of how they need help, and how he can help them. We've got to wonder if it is right for him to impose his values on people, decide what they should want and give it to them? Is that really helpful?

Apart from this he burnt easily, even an hour or so in the sun would bring up red, scaly patches about the neck and forehead and make him fretful, whereas my children had grown up in the open and thrived on it. (20.22)

Thought: Sacrabani is foreign to Ruku because he looks different from other children. In Ruku's mind, he already carries the shameful mark of being an illegitimate child – his albino deformity is just the icing on the cake. For Ruku, it's almost as if his physical strangeness is an appropriate reflection of the moral strangeness under which he was conceived.

Each night was a struggle, more fierce now that we were daily engaged in it. I saw, night after night, what I had not observed before: the lame with their crutches knocked away from them so that they fell and were unable to rise; the feeble separated from their supporters so that their numbers were halved. (27.8)

Thought: The city is foreign to Nathan and Ruku geographically, environmentally, in terms of customs. But its most glaring foreignness comes from the way it transforms people into creatures that are entirely different from people Nathan and Ruku have encountered before. Humanity as Nathan and Ruku have known it, is altered. The natural setting they once lived in fostered a natural relationship between people. In the city, people are foreign to each other, but they're also entirely foreign to human kindness. It's like they're living in an altered landscape, where the rules of humanity have changed.

He himself did not appear to find any difficulty in managing without, except that once or twice he had to use both hands, and there was a certain awkwardness in his handling of the food. Despite myself I could not keep my eyes off his hands; the harder I tried to keep my gaze fixed elsewhere, the more it fastened itself to those stumps. Puli, seemingly unaware, continued eating stolidly. He is used to it, I thought. He knows and accepts the shameful probing curiosities of human beings. (27.52)

Thought: Human beings have a natural curiosity about people that are different. Ruku doesn't judge Puli for his difference, but his experience is foreign to hers. Besides his physical deformity, which she can't help but look at, she is also enamored of Puli because he's so different from her. His can-do attitude, brashness, and self-assurance, are a comfort to Ruku because these characteristics are so foreign to her own personality. Puli's ways make him comfortable in this foreign place, which is in turn a comfort to Ruku. In a strange twist of events, she's found comfort in his foreignness.

Women and Femininity Quotes

Nathan at first paid scant attention to her: he had wanted a son to continue his line and walk beside him on the land, not a puling infant who would take with her a dowry and leave nothing but a memory behind; but soon she stopped being a puling infant, and when at the age of ten months she called him "Apa," which means father, he began to take a lively interest in her. (2.49)

Thought: As Kenny later reminds Ruku about Ira's own baby, a child is a child. Al children will no doubt engender love accordingly, regardless of the circumstances of their births. Ruku and Nathan are not excited about having a girl first, but they learn to be excited about Ira being Ira. Nathan is a loving man – he learns to love Ira just the way he learned to love Ruku. He's not one for big concern about gender roles and expectations; he loves his women in spite of what society says they should do or be.

I did so, and as soon as the door was closed the woman threw off her veil the better to select what she wanted. Her face was very pale, the bones small and fine. Her eyes were pale too, a curious light brown matching her silky hair. She took what she wanted and paid me. Her fingers, fair and slender, were laden with jeweled rings, any one of which would have fed us for a year. She smiled at me as I went out, then quickly lowered the veil again about her face. I never went there again. (8.15)

Thought: Rukmani does not feel a connection to this woman, though they are both keepers of their homes. Instead, the woman's alien culture and lifestyle are more important defining aspects in Ruku's eyes. She has culture in common with Kali, Janaki and Kunthi, and perhaps this is an important aspect of them being a community of women.

"Neighbors, women… and I a failure, a woman who cannot even bear a child."

All this I had gone through—the torment, the anxiety. Now the whole dreadful story was repeating itself, and it was my daughter this time. (9.16)

Thought: It's interesting that Ruku agrees that a woman's importance largely rests in her ability to bear a child. Ruku didn't ever overcome these feelings to find her self-worth as a woman – she got over them by bearing children. She suffers because of Ira's failure to conceive, and her only solution to Ira is not a philosophical one about a woman's greater worth. Instead, she'll seek to fix Ira's biological problem.

I was getting more and more worried about her: she moped about, dull of hair and eye, as if the sweetness of life had departed—as indeed it has for a woman who has been abandoned by her husband. (11.1)

Thought: Ruku's personal and cultural views admit that a woman's worth is largely defined by her relationship to her husband. Ira has been abandoned by her husband, and this defines her worth as a woman. Her husband leaving her affects her own views of herself, and her mother doesn't do much to ease that grief, likely because her mother understands and believes Ira is actually lessened by this abandonment.

"She is happy with the child," I replied, "but I do not know what is to become of her in the future."

"Always worrying," he chided. "It is a mercy that she is young again, should one not be grateful?"

He was a man and did not understand. (11.44)

Thought: Nathan is less burdened by cultural norms about abandoned women than Ruku is. To him, what matters foremost is Ira's happiness. He doesn't understand (or doesn't believe) that Ira's entire happiness should rest on her worth to a man. It's hard to discern though, whether he's unconcerned because he doesn't understand the full brunt of the culture's evaluation of women, or because he disagrees with it.

Under her faded sari her breasts hung loose; gone was the tense suppleness that had been her pride and her power. Of her former beauty not a vestige remained. Well, I thought, all women come to it sooner or later: she has come off perhaps worse than most. (14.17)

Thought: A woman's beauty is an aspect of her value. Ruku married below her caste in part because she wasn't a beautiful woman. Kunthi is notable because of her beauty, and ironically she sells her beauty to prostitution. Kunthi wants food because she thinks health will bring her beauty back. Ruku has never had to worry about her beauty so she seems more comfortable with the fact that beauty will go.

"Yes, of course, darling," Ira cried, and all the guilt of her efforts to have an abortion was in her voice. "I would not lose you for anything. Why do you have to ask?" (22.9)

Thought: Ruku is adding commentary here – she knows she would've traded Ira for a boy, so she can be less forgiving and gentle in her harsh (but honest) assessment of Ira's position. The love for the child is immaterial to Ruku – the important thing is that Ira's womanhood has left her in a particular societal position, and an abortion would've been preferable to being a marked woman who is also the single mother of an albino.

Ira and I did what we could; but the land is mistress to man, not to woman: the heavy work needed is beyond her strength. (23.1)

Thought: While cultural values dominate much of how women are viewed in the novel, Ruku brings up a physical reality here. It's not society, but biology, that limits Ruku and Ira when it comes to the land. While social strictures are regrettable, some of a woman's limitations are simply insurmountable.

The doctor meanwhile was approaching. Under the thin shirt I saw the figure of a woman and I whispered hastily to my husband: "Be careful—it is a woman." Nathan turned bewildered eyes on me. "The trousers—" he began, but there was no time to say more and he stopped short, confused and stammering. (25.47)

Thought: Ruku is as surprised as Nathan at the high position of this woman in their society. Here Ruku reveals that she buys into all the cultural norms about what women can and should aspire to be. A woman doctor is an aberration, and Ruku sees her as an alien creature, one to be feared (hence her warning to Nathan).

"One must live," she repeated, defiant, challenging, sensing reproach where none could be; for it is very true, one must live. (26.36)

Thought: Prostitution is a reality for women in the book, and Ruku eventually accepts it without judgment. Ruku's society's limitations on women left them few other choices when they were faced with poverty. Moral norms no longer really factor in for Ruku's regard of prostitution, as she's come too close to the practical economic reality faced by poor women. (Interestingly, many First World women that are hard-up today make the same choice.)

Power Quotes

The following week I sold almost my whole basket to him, keeping only a little for Old Granny. I did not like selling to him, although he paid me a better price. It was business and nothing else with him, never a word of chaff or a smile—or perhaps it was the flattery I missed—and I would much rather have had it the other way; but there you are, you cannot choose. (3.52)

Thought: Ruku is powerless to choose her buyer – this is the nature of business. Regardless of how she feels, she has to go to where she gets the best price. It's interesting that the money she earns gives her some economic power. Has she has given up personal power in order to earn it?

About this time Arjun was in his early teens. He was tall for his age and older than his years. I had taught him the little I knew of reading and writing; now he could've taught me and most other people in the town. (9.19)

Thought: Arjun's education will give him power, but ironically his power will only end up crippling him. His literacy allows him to lead the movement for higher wages at the tannery. His literacy is not persuasive against the tannery because there are many more people to fill the spots left empty by the strike. There are limits to the power of literacy; it cannot always assure one a higher position or greater leverage when dealing with people in power. Ultimately, literacy only gives one power to know how far one *could* go, but in this case, it does not provide the power to get there.

"I will ask Kenny to help you. White men have power."

"Indeed they have," he said bitterly. "Over men, and events, and especially over women." (9.31)

Thought: Ruku's admission is startling but true. Though they are foreign to this society, white men seem to have greater power than non-white men. Her son resents this (with reference to the tannery), but he also resents the ripple of white power over other aspects of society, especially as white people have changed the social dynamic (with regard to his belief of the rumor of his mother's infidelity with Kenny). White folks have just waltzed into their society and believed they can do what they want politically, economically, and personally.

Sandalwood paste smeared her swelling hips, under her hips were dark painted shadows which gave them sensuous depth, the nipples were tipped with red.

I released her. She stood there before me panting, with her hair shaken loose and coiling about her shoulders.

"Guard your tongue," I said, "or it will be the worse for you."

She said nothing for a moment, while she rearranged her garments, recovering herself a little; then once again that maddening, insulting half-smile curved her lips.

"And for you," she said, with knives in her voice, "and for your precious husband." (11.27)

Thought: Ruku and Kunthi are in a battle over who has greater power. Kunthi's sexuality is far more powerful than Ruku's – not only is she more beautiful than Ruku, but her body paint and nakedness seem to assert her ownership of her own body as a sexual creature. Ruku, by contrast, rests on the power of her status as an honorable married woman and mother. Kunthi represents woman's power as an object of sexual desire, while Ruku is a powerful figure of the domestic woman. That's also why Kunthi specifically threatens Ruku's family life, talking about her husband. Everyone might know Kunthi is a prostitute, so her sexual power (and social inferiority) are certain, but Ruku's power as a family woman might be more compromised by Kunthi's knowledge, both about Ruku's visits to Kenny and also about Nathan's fathering of Kunthi's children.

When a whole week had passed thus, the tannery officials called a meeting to announce that those who did not return to work would be replaced. My sons came home from that meeting even more silent, if possible, than they had been in the past. This was the test, and it failed. The next morning the tannery had its full complement again, most of them workers who had gone back, the remainder men who were only too glad to obtain employment. (12.20)

Thought: Power is often not aligned with principles. Ruku's sons have chosen to use what they think is their bargaining power to stand up against the tannery. In the end, the tannery gets its power from people whose needs compromise their principles. For the poor, the power of conviction has no chance against the power of necessity.

So we stood and argued and begged, and in the end Sivaji agreed to wait. He took the money and turned to go, then he hesitated and said, a little wistfully: "What I do I must, for I must think of my own…. I do not wish to be hard. May you prosper."

"May you prosper too," I whispered, hardly able to speak, for his words had left me defenseless. (13.69)

Thought: The power of human kindness sometimes shines through even in the darkest moments of practical reality. Sivaji has to do his job, and Ruku and Nathan condemn him for his acceptance of the cruelty his job requires. When they see Sivaji as just an agent of a remote power, they can hate him, but when he shows kindness and empathy, he reminds them that he too is just a guy struggling to make ends meet. Power is a chain, and it's easy to resent those that are right above you until you remember they too are just below someone else.

It became possible for me to speak as well. I told him of her earlier visit and the grain she had extorted from me also; and it seemed to me that a new peace came to us then, freed at last from the necessity for lies and concealment and deceit, with the fear of betrayal lifted from us, and with the power we ourselves had given wrested finally from Kunthi. (14.81)

Thought: We realize here that it wasn't Kunthi's power that was in control of Nathan and Rukmani. Actually, it was the power of their own secrets. The lies and concealment were more about Nathan and Rukmani's fear of being found out in their betrayals of each other. Kunthi only had power as a possible means by which the truth might come out, while the real power lay in the delicate lies on which Nathan and Ruku had built their relationship.

"I must know," I said, imploring. "It is better that I should know than that I should imagine."

Ira gave me a sidelong glance: "Your imagination would not travel that far." (16.45)

Thought: The power of the imagination is greater than the power of the truth. Ruku labors under not knowing the truth, and so her imagination is allowed to run wild, ultimately leading her to darker things than even might be true. Ira, by withholding the actual truth, has power over her mother and forces her mother to imagine the worst.

"It is a long time since," she said. "You had better have a meal here before you go." She called to the servant and spoke to him rapidly, and he came, looking none too pleased, to lead us to where we had to go. (25.63)

Thought: It's interesting that the lower classes seem to begrudge each other a little help. The servants at the doctor's house initially tried to shoo away Nathan and Rukmani, taking them for beggars. The servants continue to be disdainful, and it's only the doctor, who is better off than all of them, who offers a little charity. There's no empathy among the poor, perhaps because they're struggling to be better off than *somebody*, perhaps because they see each other as competitors, or perhaps because familiarity breeds contempt.

Yet I thought, what I did not wish to think, of the time when the disease that had claimed his fingers would creep up, eating away his limbs—or attack some other part, his feet or his eyes. What then of this bright fearless child who boasted that he stood alone? There is a limit to the achievements of human courage. (27.132)

Thought: Puli may have power over how he approaches the world, but in the end, he is powerless to stand up against his disease. No amount of street smarts can save him from his illness. If he's going to be saved, he needs to submit to the help of others. (This is particularly painful for him because he is continually proud he is of being able to take care of himself.) Still, sometimes it's more courageous to ask for help than to stubbornly do things on your own, especially if not asking for help means certain death from leprosy.

Plot Analysis

Classic Plot Analysis

Initial Situation
Rukmani marries Nathan and moves to his modest home to start a life and family.
This is one of the best times in Rukmani's life. Her marriage is underway, and her husband, Nathan, is kind to her. Rukmani and her husband are full of hope for the future: Nathan will eventually be able to buy their land, and Rukmani will raise a happy healthy family, who will take on the legacy of farming. The family is also established in this period – Rukmani gives birth to Ira, and eventually five more sons in rapid succession. Though times are a bit tight, this period is generally characterized by a hopeful feeling of promise and potential.

Conflict
Rukmani struggles to keep her family afloat through monsoon, drought, starvation, and general poverty.
Each member of Ruku's family faces his or her own challenges and deals with them individually. Arjun and Thambi leave for Ceylon, abandoning their family; Murugan leaves his family for a servant job in the city; Raja, weak from starvation, is killed while he is stealing from the tannery; Ira is abandoned by her husband, returns home, and turns to prostitution to feed Kuti; Kuti dies of starvation and sickness, and Ruku and Nathan struggle through starvation and fear of betrayal before admitting that neither of them has been completely honest.

All of these personal conflicts take place against the backdrop of Ruku and Nathan's greater conflict with the land. Their livelihood is threatened by monsoon and drought, causing crops to fail in one way or another, and resulting in starvation. This poverty informs the personal conflicts of the characters, but also serves as an umbrella of the general difficulties that the entire family faces under harsh conditions.

Complication
When Selvam decides to work with Kenny, we learn that every last one of Nathan and Rukmani's children have deserted the family's traditional livelihood in one way or another.
When Selvam decides to work with Kenny, it's the last nail in the coffin for Ruku and Nathan's hope that they might keep the land and prosper on it. Selvam's decision means that Ruku and Nathan can only keep the land for as long as Nathan can work; Ruku talks with Kenny about the fact that they do not have the luxury of planning, as they can never anticipate what will happen

next.

Climax

Nathan and Rukmani find out their land is being sold to the tannery. They must leave the land they've been on for thirty years.

This is the point of no return in the novel. The land is gone, their livelihood is gone, and there is no hope of keeping the home they've made together. Ruku and Nathan have lost their battle against the merciless reality of subsistence living.

Suspense

Nathan and Rukmani set out to find Murugan, encountering many hardships along the way.

Selvam, Ira and Sacrabani will figure out some way to carry on, and only Rukmani and Nathan will leave. They set out to the city with high hopes – they know that if they find Murugan, he will keep them and assure they are taken care of. Their quest for Murugan is populated with little setbacks, especially the theft of their goods and money. Still, they hope they will find Murugan and once again have a home.

Denouement

Nathan and Rukmani discover that Murugan has fled his family and his job. Later, the leprous street boy joins the two travelers, Puli, who leads them to a job in the stone quarry that helps them earn enough money to go home.

Nathan and Ruku finally find Murugan's home, only to learn there is no more Murugan. It's clear from their daughter-in-law Ammu's living conditions that they cannot stay with her. They settle into a life of homeless poverty in the temple and begin to nurse hopes of returning to their village, even though they know they'll be in poverty there too. Puli helps them get the money to make this happen. Even though they'll be getting out of the city, it's rather anticlimactic that they'll only go back to the village (and the poverty) that is familiar to them. Though it's not much solace, at least they'll be going back to their home village and family.

Conclusion

Nathan dies in the nameless city. Rukmani returns home to her village and remaining children with Puli in tow.

Nathan doesn't make it, but Ruku finds her family again and announces that Puli is now a part of it. The family still struggles, but Ruku is now more of an observer than a participant. Her time is over, and the time for her children, who will likely struggle as she did before them, has arrived.

Booker's Seven Basic Plots Analysis: Rebirth

Booker's plot structure doesn't perfectly fit this novel because the story is not told in a usual style leading up to a single end or climatic event. There are elements of "The Quest," "Tragedy," and "Voyage and Return," but none is a single guiding aspect of Ruku's life; instead, these are fairly incidental to the arch of the plot.

"Rebirth" is perhaps the most appropriate for this book among Booker's plots, but even this classification is problematic. Arguably, not much has changed over the course of the narration. Ruku's story is comprised of one hardship after another, and only punctuated sporadically with

the little joys that characterize a typical rebirth story.

But we are hesitant to put it into this category because the rebirth trope relies on some miraculous redemption by another happening at the end of the story. There is no such miraculous intervention (though Rukmani does find a savior in Puli), and when she returns to her life in the village, the reader knows she will face the same struggles and difficulties she had known in the past. Ultimately, this is story of how Rukmani acquired grace and quiet acceptance in the face of great hardship. Unlike the rebirth trope, what's most important is how Ruku has stayed her steady self in spite of all hardships. Her triumph in the end is not that she is born again, but simply that she continues to live.

Three Act Plot Analysis

Act I
Rukmani and Nathan must finally give up on their land as their plot is being sold to the tannery. They must leave to the city to find their son Murugan and a new life.

Act II
Rukmani and Nathan are destitute and homeless in Murugan's city. They discover that there son is nowhere to be found: he has deserted his wife (and by extension, his parents). They have nowhere to turn and are left with no means to either support themselves or return home.

Act III
Rukmani and Nathan earn a little money to return to the village. Nathan dies before they get there. Rukmani goes back to the village with Puli, and Selvam and Ira greet them. Her children will have to figure out how to create a new life.

Study Questions

1. Why does Markandaya avoid talking about any specifics of time and place in the novel? What does she accomplish by avoiding anchoring the novel in practical details? Is the story any more universal for lack of these details?
2. In times of utter desperation Rukmani turns to the gods, to her husband, to Kenny, and to others. How dependent is Ruku on other people and outside forces? On the other hand, what indications do we have about her self-reliance?
3. Rukmani despairs to learn that her first child is a girl. What does she feel about her own position as a woman? When she refers to her own feelings, how much does her femininity factor into how much agency she has? How does she regard women differently than men?
4. Why is the narrative told as a flashback? What's up with the moments in the narrative that Rukmani tells in the present tense, namely Raja's death, her travel away from her village, and Nathan's death?
5. How present is colonialism in the narrative? Is it an issue of race, of power, of modernity?

Why is India's colonial transition never specifically referenced? Is Markandaya implicitly discussing colonialism by using individual characters and objects (like Kenny, and the tannery) as metaphors or stereotypes?

Characters

All Characters

Rukmani Character Analysis

Rukmani is a hard-working and supportive wife, daughter, and mother, who grows and develops over the course of the novel. She is our sole narrator, and as such she exercises tremendous power over the reader. What is perhaps most interesting about her is that in spite of the fact that she has full control over the narration, she seems to be a fairly honest narrator. She admits her failures and weaknesses.

It is through seeing Rukmani's shortcomings, that we realize her strengths: her honesty gives her a true grace and humility. Ultimately, we realize Rukmani is faced with a world that is beyond her control and understanding. She does her best to endure, for her family and for herself. She provides support to Nathan and cares for her children, but she is also engaged in a project of learning. She breaks caste restrictions when she allows her sons to work at the tannery, and she becomes immune to the realities of poverty when she sees three women around her involved in prostitution. When she returns home to her modest village life at the end of the novel – with one more mouth to feed, but strong as ever in her faith to survive – we see she has come a far way from being the little girl who quaked at the possibility of living in a two-room mud hut.

Throughout the novel Rukmani has learned to be more generous, less judgmental, and to identify the things that really matter to her. Ultimately, she proves the wisdom of the advice Nathan gave her early on – to not break, but to bend like the grass.

As a result of her endurance and faithful commitment to keep going on no matter what, Rukmani is like the character Sita, the wife of Rama in the Indian epic, the *Ramayan*. Sita was noted for being a faithful and loving wife, and she withstood rumors about her fidelity (as Ruku does) and incredible hardship (as Ruku also does). Ultimately, also like Ruku, Sita returns to the land from whence she came: Sita is swallowed up by the earth, the way Rukmani faces death after returning to the place she most loves.

Rukmani Timeline and Summary

- When we first encounter Rukmani, she is an old woman at home with her family. Having just lost her husband, she begins to look back over her life.
- She fills us in on her childhood: she was the last of four daughters, and though her father was an important man in her village, he couldn't afford a large dowry.
- Rukmani has a simple marriage to Nathan, a poor tenant farmer. She is twelve at the time of her wedding.
- Rukmani is sickened and saddened by leaving her family, but Nathan cheers her on the ride home. Her heart sinks more when she sees the simple life she'll have in a very modest mud hut beside a paddy field.
- Still, Rukmani eventually settles in comfortably to her new village life, making friends with the local women and learning their ways.
- Rukmani is particularly proud of her vegetable garden, where she raises a pumpkin that she shows with pride to Nathan.
- Rukmani helps her neighbor Kunthi as the woman gives birth. Ruku stays on for some time because the midwife did not arrive.
- Rukmani does less and less work outside as her own pregnancy proceeds. She now devotes more time to her reading and writing, excited to teach these skills to her children. Rukmani is also pleased with Nathan's reaction to her literacy: her husband is proud, and not resentful, of his wife's education.
- Rukmani gives birth to a baby girl. She weeps at the sight of the child for she had wished for a boy, believing that girls are only a burden.
- Rukmani grows happier with her new daughter, Ira.
- It's been six years since Rukmani gave birth to Ira, and she is increasingly worried that she will have no more children.
- She often goes to temple with her mother to pray, and she carries a good luck charm, but to no avail.
- As Rukmani tends to her dying mother, she meets a British doctor named Kenny.
- Prompted by Kenny, Rukmani finally pours her heart out about her sadness at having only one child, and a daughter at that.
- At first, Rukmani shrinks from Kenny's offer of help. Since nothing else works, she finally goes to Kenny for fertility treatment.
- Rukmani gives birth to her first child in seven years and is thrilled that it's a boy.
- At the celebration, Rukmani looks for Kenny and is disappointed he isn't there. She notes that she still hasn't told Nathan about Kenny's help with the fertility treatment and is worried that he'll be angry with her for keeping it from him in the first place.
- Rukmani gives birth to four more sons, making six children in all (five boys and Ira).
- To make a little extra money, Rukmani begins selling the vegetables she grows.
- At first Rukmani sells her vegetables to Old Granny, a homeless woman who lives in the village. Ruku soon switches to Biswas, the moneylender, because he gives her a better price. Our heroine notes times are getting tighter at home. Her family, however, always manages to make do.
- Rukmani saves a little bit at a time and eventually creates a dowry for Ira.
- When she learns that a tannery will be built near her farm, Ruku bemoans this turn of

events. She realizes that the tannery may change the environment and economy of the village for the worse.
- Rukmani runs into Kenny while she is out collecting dung for fuel and repairs.
- She listens as Kenny says the earth would benefit from the dung, but she quietly points out that her family needs the dung's benefits too.
- Rukmani welcomes Kenny into her home to have the midday meal with her family. As Kenny warmly congratulates Nathan on all their children, she worries that Kenny will reveal the secret of her fertility treatment, which she still hasn't mentioned to her husband. She's relieved when Kenny fails to go into details.
- Rukmani prepares an arranged marriage for Ira. She chooses Old Granny to make the match. Ruku she is pleased that Old Granny doesn't have hard feelings about the fact that Rukmani stopped selling her vegetables.
- Once Old Granny has found a nice match for Ira, Rukmani wistfully remembers her own marriage. She assures Ira that she'll be fine once she settles into her new life as a wife. Rukmani also reflects sadly on the fact that Ira's position as a wife will now trump her position as a daughter.
- Rukmani puts on a modest but joyful wedding for Ira, bringing out the stores of food she's been saving.
- Rukmani notes that Ira looks too young to be going off with a husband.
- Terrible rains strike just after Ira's marriage. Ruku does her best to keep her home comfortable in the midst of this unfortunate change in the weather.
- After the rain blows over, Ruku tries to calculate how they'll fix up their house. She has to refuse help to her neighbor, Kali, as her resources are already so stretched.
- One day following the rains, Rukmani goes to the market to stock up on provisions, but returns empty-handed, because no one had anything to sell. She lays awake listening to the drums of calamity beating over the village.
- Rukmani sets out again with Nathan the next day. After a haggle, the couple buys two pounds of rice with all their money, leaving nothing left for repairs.
- Rukmani eventually works with her family, harvesting fish from the fields and helping to salvage the paddy. They stay up late cleaning fish and separating rice grains from the husk. Rukmani dreams of feeding her family with new vegetables.
- Rukmani has a bit of a tiff with her neighbor, Kunthi, who has grown distant. Ruku chides Kunthi for not being a creature of the earth, suggesting she'd be better off if she were more humble and modest.
- Rukmani also notes that yet another neighbor, Janaki, is in trouble. The neighbor's family has had to leave their home; Ruku can't help or think about them, so she pushes it from her mind, focusing on her own troubles.
- Rukmani marvels at the Muslims that are working at the tannery and living in their own area of the village. She does business with one Muslim woman, and is troubled by the woman's isolation. She decides never to return to the woman's house.
- Rukmani despairs for Ira when her husband returns her to the family home. Her husband claims that because she has not fulfilled her wifely duty of bearing children, and hence is no wife. Rukmani laments because she went through the same thing.
- Rukmani also faces the difficulty of her two eldest sons' decision to work in the tannery. She's hurt by the suggestion that Arjun makes that the family isn't working hard enough to provide for everyone. She's especially hurt by Arjun's suggestion that there's something going on between her and Kenny.

- Still, Ruku uses the money her sons bring in from the tannery. She buys clothes and food, and she fixes the roof damaged by the storm.
- Rukmani celebrates Deepavali with her family, even buying the children extravagances like firecrackers.
- She has a great night on her own, and when she comes home, she and her husband make passionate love.
- Rukmani later visits Kenny to ask for fertility help with Ira.
- On the way home from her late visit with Kenny, Ruku runs into Kunthi on the road. The two get into a fracas, and Rukmani tears at Kunthi's sari, only to realize that Kunthi wears the marks of a prostitute. She threatens Kunthi to keep her mouth shut about her visit to Kenny, but the encounter leaves her shaken.
- Ruku goes to ask Ira's husband to take her back. Sadly, it's too late: he's re-married and can no longer take Ira back.
- Ironically, it is Rukmani who becomes pregnant again. She gives birth to a tiny baby boy that she names Kuti.
- Rukmani remains troubled about Ira's future. She talks to Old Granny and worries Ira will end a poor woman, old and alone.
- Rukmani realizes her sons are behind a strike in the tannery. She rails against their futile efforts to fight their bosses and can't understand why they don't just accept the status quo, grateful for what little they get.
- When it becomes clear that the two oldest sons can no longer go back to the tannery, they decide to leave home for work. Rukmani has to accept that her sons are leaving; as they pack up and make her empty promises, she's sure she'll never see them again.
- Rukmani is brought out, and gains a little refreshment, from looking at the paddy fields with Nathan. She is drawn into hopeful planning about the future with him. Still, she notes the village is not as beautiful as it once was.
- Later, Kenny visits and brings good news of Murugan, her son who left to be employed as a servant in the city.
- Rukmani suddenly feels brave, and she inquires whether Kenny doesn't have his own family and home.
- She is quickly embarrassed by her brashness.
- As Kenny reveals his own past, Rukmani promises she'll never reveal it to anyone. She insists she isn't a gossip. She watches with curiosity as he slinks away.
- At one point in the novel it becomes clear that Ruku and Nathan will have difficulty paying their rent. Rukmani stands by Nathan as Nathan haggles with Sivaji, the landlord's messenger. She tries to comfort Nathan in his despair, reminding her husband that the man before them is only doing his job.
- Rukmani gathers all the things she can think of to sell in order to keep the land.
- Once Ruku has decided what must be sold, she visits Biswas, the cruel moneylender, to sell her goods. She haggles and bluffs with him, eventually battling him up to 75 rupees from his initial offer of 30.
- Rukmani returns home and has a rare fight with Nathan: he wants to sell their remaining seed, but she thinks they'd be unwisely selling off their future for the sake of the present.
- The next day when Sivaji comes by to collect there's another haggle. Rukmani is softened, when the rent collector points out that he's only doing what he must and wishes that their family might prosper.
- Rukmani worries about how her family will eat. She pulls out her final reserve of rice, and

counts it out into small portions that will feed everyone for 24 days.

- Kunthi shows up and has a squabble with Ruku again, this time demanding food. As Kunthi threatens to reveal Ruku's visits with Kenny to Nathan, Ruku temporarily loses her senses. She has some misgivings, realizing that not even her genuine fidelity can protect her. She has misled Nathan about some things, namely the treatment she received from Kenny, and wonders if her husband will incorrectly assume that she has lied about other things as well.
- Ruku doesn't know what else to do, and in despair she gives Kunthi seven days worth of rice rations.
- Ruku later goes back to count what's left of the rice, and finds that only about one day's worth of rice remains.
- She panics and flips out, and rushes in to accuse her children of stealing the rice.
- When Rukmani hears Nathan's admission that he took the rice, she's shocked.
- She's even more shocked to learn that Nathan is the father of two of Kunthi's sons.
- She quickly calms down when she and Nathan get the chance to discuss everything openly. Ruku and Nathan finally admit their deceptions to each other.
- Rukmani is relieved that Kunthi no longer has power over them, but she knows now they'll face starvation.
- Rukmani coolly describes the starvation that grips her family.
- Next, our heroine must bravely face two men as they bring home her son, Raja's, dead body.
- Rukmani is shocked to hear them explain what happened. She chastises Ira for wasting her tears, but then Ira's sorrow flows into her.
- Rukmani observes Raja's body with a cool despair. She pleads with God, asking if this is why her son was brought into the world. She tends to his body, and notes that his spirit is gone. The work she does now is for this body, not for his soul.
- Rukmani stands aside at the preparation for Raja's funeral, and the men carry his body away for cremation.
- Rukmani listens to the drums beat during the cremation – she knows at the last drumbeat that Raja's body is gone.
- Three days later, Rukmani deals with two men visiting from the tannery who have arrived to explain the unfortunate death.
- She's perplexed by their bizarre visit: they have come to get her to agree the tannery has no liability in Raja's death.
- Rukmani thinks this is silly because there is no possible compensation for her son's death. Nothing can replace her son, not even the tannery's money.
- Rukmani comforts the smaller of the two men who seems to be taking the visit rather hard. With detachment, she assures him it does not matter, as not much really matters to her now.
- Rukmani is in bed one night when she hears a woman's footsteps approach.
- Thinking it is her neighbor, Kunthi, coming to steal the last of what they have, Ruku throws herself at the woman in the night.
- Her husband Nathan pulls her off of the woman. Ruku realizes with shock that the nightwalker was not Kunthi, but her own daughter, Ira.
- She tends to Ira's wounds, and then wash Ira's sari, only to watch a rupee fall from it into the river.
- Rukmani tries to talk to Ira about what she's doing and why, but can't get anywhere.

Ruku can only imagine the many debasements Ira endures in the streets as a prostitute.

- Rukmani turns her attention to Kuti, her littlest baby and youngest son, who has been suffering immensely from starvation.
- She is with him, trying to comfort him up until the very last moment when he dies.
- Holding his dead body, she notes that she doesn't wish him back to life, as there is only suffering for him on earth.
- Ironically, Rukmani soon rejoices with her family as they put work into harvesting the seed that has finally blossomed, and capture ample fish from the fields. They all excitedly make plans for the future.
- Rukmani hears from Biswas, the cruel moneylender, that Kenny has returned.
- Ruku visits Kenny. They have a pleasant meeting, although they talk about the dark times that have just passed.
- Rukmani tells Kenny that two of her sons have died, and her daughter is pregnant with a stranger's baby, after turning to prostitution.
- Rukmani doesn't warm up to Kenny's suggestion that everything will be fine once the baby is born.
- Walking home, Rukmani thinks about what Kenny said about the baby and notes that Nathan shares Kenny's view. She is comforted by the possibility that the two men are right.
- Back at home, Rukmani listens as Selvam announces he will no longer work on the land. Instead, has decided to take a job with Kenny at the new hospital under construction.
- After some prodding, Rukmani admits that she's a bit disappointed: Selvam's decision means none of her sons will work the land.
- Still, she is happy for Selvam, and knows that this is the best thing for him.
- Rukmani thinks about warning Selvam that some people will suggest that he got the job because of the rumored "special relationship" between her and Kenny. She decides not to damper his spirits with such talk.
- Mother and son have a quiet moment of complete understanding, and Ruku accepts Selvam's assurance that he trusts her, and that she need only trust herself.
- Ruku visits Kenny and thanks him for the favor to Selvam.
- While talking to Kenny, she sees the plans for the new hospital and inquires about funding.
- Rukmani is bewildered, not understanding why people who don't know her village would want to help them.
- Rukmani thinks to herself that man's wants are eternal and inevitable – man's spirits are given to him not to beg, but to rise above his desires.
- Our narrator tells Kenny that the village priests teach them to suffer and endure, as it's cleansing for the spirit. The two then have a discussion about the place of suffering in humanity.
- Rukmani prepares to help Ira give birth.
- As she makes all the logistical arrangements, she wonders over the many births that the house has seen.
- Ruku also ruminates on her concerns about this baby: without a proper father, there's no guarantee this baby will be a safe and normal one.
- Our narrator notices immediately that Ira's baby is albino. She's shocked and dismayed that Ira seems totally obliviousness to the weirdness of the baby.
- Rukmani tries to make the best of a bad situation and points out to Nathan that their daughter is happy.

- Still, Rukmani is disturbed by the baby's transparency in the sun. She has a hard time adopting to the differences between this baby and other children.
- Rukmani finally accepts that bemoaning their fate and trying to lay blame is futile.
- At one point in the novel, Ruku reflects on the building of the hospital. She informs us that at the time, no one knew it would take seven years to finish the building.
- We discover that Old Granny has died of starvation. Ruku is pained because she could have helped the woman. Rather than offer to help, Rukmani actually accepted Old Granny's last rupee as a gift for Ira's baby, Sacrabani. Still, she ruminates on the fact that no one paid attention to Old Granny's suffering in life because no one could afford to add her troubles to theirs.
- The entire village takes care of the funeral arrangements for Old Granny.
- Rukmani is already wary – people have begun to plague her to see if they can get spots at the hospital once it's built. It's clear to even her that only a few of the people that need help will be helped by the hospital. There's just too much need.
- Rukmani tries to follow along with the fundraising and financial planning Kenny and Selvam do. She is still baffled, however, because she believes there is not enough money or compassion in the world to help all who are in need.
- Rukmani watches as Sacrabani begins to ask his mother difficult questions; he wants to know what it means to be a bastard, and where his father is.
- Rukmani doesn't offer any help during Ira's talk with her child. After Sacrabani leaves the Ruku tells Ira it might have been better to tell the child his father was dead.
- Ira leaves the hut, clearly distraught, but Rukmani chooses not to follow her.
- Instead, she listens to Ira weep once Nathan goes out to her.
- As the novel progresses, Rukmani tends to Nathan in his ailing health. She can't help but worry that he needs to get better: the whole family relies on him being a breadwinner.
- One day, Rukmani talks with Kenny frankly about their situation, and notes that their sons have all made their own way. She says they're all in God's hands.
- Rukmani comes home one day to find Nathan in a state of shock.
- Hearing the news that their land is to be sold, Rukmani is shocked too. Surrounded by what she considers madness, Rukmani is unable to talk about the immense thing that has happened.
- Rukmani has a few moments where she reflects on the tannery. She reasons that this business has brought nothing good. Still, she admits it once brought her family prosperity. She also recognizes that the land is also to blame for their ills, unreliable and unpredictable as it has always been.
- Later, Rukmani is mostly quiet, while she watches her son and husband discuss what there is to do. She is hurt by Nathan's insistence that he's a broken old man. Nathan is a source of great comfort to her, however, because she realizes they need each other now more than ever. She reckons with the fact that they really have no choice but to go to her son, Murugan, in the city.
- Rukmani is full of nostalgia as she packs up her last few items and prepares for the journey to the city. She gathers what little money they have, and she and Nathan saddle up together, waving goodbye to their family.
- Once Nathan and Ruku reach the city, they realize they are not sure of how to find Murugan. They grow increasingly tired and lost, bewildered by the big city.
- They stop to have a snack and a rest, and by the time they have strength enough to travel, it's too dark to do anything.

- They go to a temple for food and shelter.
- Rukmani tries to pray, and at first she can only concentrate on her family and all she's left behind. Finally, she settles into prayer.
- When the time comes for the sharing of the food offering, Rukmani finds a place within the jostling crowd. She handles some ridicule for trying to collect her and Nathan's portion. In the end, they are forced to share one portion.
- After eating, they note that their bundles have disappeared. They begin to search for their lost possessions, but slowly realize that their search is in vain.
- Rukmani is irritated by the ease with which Nathan accepts the loss. All she can think of is the fact that she'll go to her daughter-in-law like a beggar. She resolves to buy some things to bring to her daughter-in-law's house.
- As Ruku sleeps fitfully, she feels things rustling against her. She dismisses it as nothing, but can't go back to sleep. She stays up marveling at the statues in the temple.
- They next morning, Rukmani and Nathan realize that thy were robbed during the night.
- They set out again to find Murugan, steeling themselves for more hunger.
- At one moment during the journey, they watch some street children play.
- Rukmani notes that the children are content enough, but seem to become animals once a scrap of food is dropped. One of the children, a boy named Puli, offers to help them find Murugan's house.
- Ruku follows Puli, their newfound guide, who he has lost his fingers to disease.
- Nathan and Ruku are under the impression that Murugan is still employed by a doctor. When they arrive at the house where Murugan should be employed, Ruku lets Nathan do the talking.
- Stunned by the fact that the doctor is a woman, Nathan stammers too much. Ruku immediately picks up his slack and explains why they are there.
- Ruku and the doctor exchange questions: Ruku hears that Murugan now works for a Collector, while the doctor gets news of Kenny and the hospital.
- Rukmani is pleasantly surprised by the doctor's generosity: they have been invited to have dinner at her servant, Das's house. The warmth she finds with Das's wife even more pleasantly surprises Ruku. Rukmani is glad to be with such a happy, warm, young family again, and finds them to be a true breath of fresh air.
- Ruku (as narrator) flips to the present for a second. To this day, she says, she likes to imagine Das's wife as she was then, smiling and happy.
- Nathan and Ruku set off to the Collector's House, and are excited at the prospect of seeing their son and new daughter-in-law.
- Unfortunately, they receive a rather cool greeting from Ammu, Murugan's wife. Nathan and Ruku can both sense from the coolness of Ammu's welcome, and both are shocked as the girl explains that her husband left her two years ago.
- Ammu definitely doesn't have resources to keep them. Rukmani accepts without the least bit of hesitation that Ammu had to turn to prostitution in order to support herself.
- Rukmani is temporarily shaken, though, by Ammu's open anger for her son. She feels the need to defend him, and suggests that perhaps he had his reasons for abandoning his wife. She apologizes for this quickly, realizing they're all in a difficult situation.
- Rukmani notes sadly that after they leave, she'll likely never see this daughter-in-law and these children again.
- Rukmani and Nathan settle back into temple life and make plans about how they'll return to their village. Rukmani has the hopeful idea that she can set up as a letter writer in the

marketplace to make some money.
- Ruku makes a bit of money, but business isn't so good.
- One day Ruku is followed to the temple by the street boy, Puli. (He's the one who showed the couple how to find Murugan in the first place.)
- The boy stays with them at the temple, and Ruku worries that he should return to his parents.
- When he says he has no parents, Ruku feels the tug to take care of him, though she knows she does not have the resources to do so.
- Puli suggests that Rukmani and Nathan look for work at the nearby stone quarry. Ruku is glad for the work and makes the best of it.
- Rukmani again makes hopeful plans with Nathan, calculating their return home. Still, she worries about what will happen to Puli as his leprosy worsens. The three settle into a lifestyle where they work at the quarry by day and sleep at the temple by night.
- One day, Rukmani walks back from work with Puli. On the way, she stops at a vendor.
- Ruku decides to spend more money at the market than usual. She reasons that they made a good amount that day, and almost have enough to return home.
- Ruku spends more on food, and continues with some extravagances when she buys two toy pull-carts, one for Puli and one for Sacrabani.
- Rukmani is a little ashamed, and panicked about what Nathan will say of these extravagances, but when she gets to the temple, she's more concerned about his sudden illness.
- She chastises him for working all day even though he was sick. She tries, to no avail, to get him to stay at the temple days. It is raining and Nathan is clearly not in good health, but he stubbornly refuses to stay at the temple.
- Ruku works in the rain for nearly seven days with Nathan beside her. One day as she walks back alone from work, she sees a big crowd gathered.
- She is called over because the crowd is surrounding her husband, who has fallen.
- She tries to wrap her sari around him, but the clothe is so frail that this is useless.
- Rukmani later recounts that she remembers every detail of this painful night.
- She follows behind as Nathan is carried to the temple, and remembers only that she kept screaming like a mad woman, "Fire cannot burn in water."
- Ruku is eventually left alone with her husband, holding his head in her lap. It becomes clear he's going to die.
- Ruku grieves deeply and explains that if she grieves it is only for herself, as she is losing her love and her life.
- Still, as he passes, Ruku promises him they've always been happy together.
- Rukmani turns to Puli to ease her grief over losing Nathan.
- She promises him that his health will improve if he returns with her to the village.
- Rukmani returns to her village with Puli, announcing to her children that she and Nathan had adopted the little boy.
- Rukmani is reassured by Selvam's and Ira's reactions. She tells her son that his father passed gently, and they'll talk about it later.

Nathan Character Analysis

Ruku says she always called her husband "husband," because calling him by his first name would be inappropriate in her culture. For the purposes of her narrative, though, she calls him Nathan.

Nathan is a tenant farmer who labors his whole life on land he doesn't own. He's the loving and wise husband of Rukmani. Nathan begins in the novel as a hopeful young man – he dreams of one day owning his own land, and he constantly points Rukmani towards the rice, which hold the seeds of their hope and future. Like Rukmani, Nathan goes to the earth for replenishment, finding a spiritual anchor there.

Nathan is gentle and loving with his wife and children, but he does go to emotional extremes that Ruku doesn't often reach. At Deepavali, he is comfortable being simply joyful, without the thought of anything else. On the other hand, he's capable of abrupt moments of incredible anger, as when he pulls Rukmani off of Ira, or when he declares that his sons must act for their benefit, or when he curses Sivaji and the Zemindar. Nathan is capable of feeling deeply, whether love or anger. His feelings give him strength and often give Rukmani pause to think.

Rukmani is still in control of the story, so we don't get Nathan's personal reflections on his life, but we have a sense of what he believes, and that he holds deeply to those convictions. He is ashamed of his infidelity with Kunthi, he refuses to eat the food brought in by Ira's prostitution; and when his life is brought to a close, he embraces the notion that happiness has been the most important part of it. In the novel, if Ruku represents thought, then Nathan is feeling. He faces strife constantly, and he endures it with a quiet acceptance, valuing what he's got over what he'll never have.

Nathan Timeline and Summary

- Nathan marries the young Rukmani, and they go to live in the modest village home that he built with his own hands. During the ride he comforts and cheers her, and does so again when she seems dispirited upon seeing their new mud-hut.
- Nathan, a farmer, praises Rukmani for the single pumpkin she's grown on her own.
- Nathan looks on as Rukmani practices her reading and writing. At first, he says nothing, but after taking a little time to think about it, Nathan praises Ruku for her cleverness.
- One day, Nathan kills the cobra Ruku chanced upon in the vegetable garden. He's unconcerned with the supposed sacredness of the cobra; he thinks mostly of protecting his pregnant wife.
- Nathan pays little attention to their daughter, Irawaddy, until she calls "Father" at the age of just ten months.
- After many years of patient waiting, Nathan is overjoyed at the arrival of their first son. He invites everyone in the village to come to a celebration at their house on the tenth day after the boy's birth.
- When first introduced to the tannery, Nathan assures Rukmani that the tannery is here to

stay. He encourages her to go with the flow, saying "Bend like the grass, that you do not break." (4.20)
- Nathan welcomes Kenny into his home, saying he's honored by Kenny's presence in his poor home.
- Nathan stoically notes that, with the monsoon drowning the paddy fields, there will be little harvest to eat this season.
- Nathan prepares to go to the market with Rukmani, counting out two rupees from their life savings for food and repairs.
- Nathan takes Ira's return home in stride – he says her husband was patient for as long as he could be expected to be.
- Nathan tries to dissuade his second son, Thambi, from working at the tannery, saying he looked forward to the time when his sons would work with him on the land. Thambi crushes his hopes by pointing out that Nathan never did, and never will, own the land.
- Nathan celebrates Deepavali joyously, parading around his sons and celebrating his wife. He returns home in high spirits and makes love to Rukmani.
- Nathan bears the results of the strike at the tannery more graciously than anyone. He declares that their children must do what they do for their benefit, not for their parents. He quiets everyone with his authority.
- Nathan is not surprised when his sons come home and announce their intention to go to Ceylon.
- Nathan does his best to comfort Rukmani now that three of their sons have left for work abroad. He brings her out to look at the beauty of paddy fields, and he talks of plans for the future.
- Nathan has to haggle and argue with Sivaji, when payment is due for the land he rents. The crops failed in the drought, so the family has no money with which to pay. Nathan finally gets Sivaji to agree they'll pay half the rent now, and the rest will follow.
- Nathan is despairing and angry. He curses men like Sivaji, who are employed to protect wealthy landowners from realizing the suffering they inflict on others.
- Nathan sells the portion of their goods they can to make up half the rent. However, they still come up short of the half they'd promised to pay.
- Rukmani and Nathan fight about whether they should sell their remaining seed. He is most concerned about paying off their present debts. Ruku convinces her husband, however, that they cannot pay for the present with the future.
- One day, Nathan rushes into his house to find Rukmani wildly accusing their children of stealing rice.
- He breaks down and admits that he stole the rice, but not for himself.
- Nathan then confesses that he is the father of two of Kunthi's children, and he was forced to give her rice when she threatened to tell Rukmani the truth.
- As Nathan tells the truth about his own infidelity, he listens to Ruku tell of her own deceptions regarding her fertility treatment. At this point, they become free of their respective lies and are closer than ever.
- Nathan suffers with the family, scavenging what little they can, and continually being optimistic about the coming harvests.
- One evening Nathan notices that Rukmani is beating their daughter, Ira. He rushes out of the hut in the middle of the night to pull Rukmani off their daughter.
- Nathan is furious at Ruku for not recognizing Ira, and he pushes her away as she tries to help.

- He holds back on questioning Ira about her night-walking until she's better.
- Then one night, as Nathan is coming back from the fields, Ira on her way out to find "work". He stops his daughter, and asks her what she thinks she's doing. He forbids her prostitution in vain, and then gets angrier, calling her out as a common strumpet. He is powerless to stop her though, and lets her pass into the night. Nathan refuses to eat anything brought in with the money from Ira's prostitution, though Ruku keeps pointing out that there's nothing they can do to stop her. Nathan continues to starve out of a sense of shame.
- There's finally a good harvest, and Nathan and his family work to collect the fish and rice from the field. They sit in an absurd joy, laughing at their past misfortune and facing the future with disbelief and optimism, once again full of plans.
- Nathan is particularly disturbed by the birth of Ira's baby Sacrabani. He was never pleased about Ira's choice to prostitute herself, and is furious that she seems indifferent to the evident strangeness of the baby. He fears she has given up her sanity to pretend her child is normal.
- Nathan blames himself for letting all of this happen.
- Nathan notes the baby is not normal, that it loves the darkness. He says this dark affinity is for bats and snakes and jackals, but not human babies.
- Nathan decides they'll have a naming ceremony, as is customary. However, rather than celebration, his motive is to stop the visitors who come and ogle the baby.
- Nathan scolds Rukmani for dwelling on Old Granny's death, and for lamenting that the hospital hadn't been built in time to save her. Nathan notes that the hospital will be for the sick, not the old.
- Nathan tries to deal gently with the difficulty Ira has in answering questions from her son about his father. He says it's Ira's choice to do as she sees fit, but he is gentle.
- Nathan leaves Ira alone for a while after she walks out, but eventually he goes to comfort her.
- He stays with her while she weeps.
- Approaching 50, Nathan is plagued by rheumatism and fevers.
- As he finally begins to get better, the news falls that his rented land is being sold to the tannery.
- He is in a state of shock, telling Ruku they must leave in two weeks.
- Later that night, Nathan tells his son, Selvam, about the sale of the land.
- Ignoring Selvam's fury, Nathan announces that they will have to stay with their son, Murugan in the city. Nathan reasons that he is too old to rent and work another plot of land.
- In an act of self-sacrifice, Nathan refuses Selvam's offer to give up his job with Kenny in order to work with his father to rent a new plot of land. Nathan insists that his son pursue the building of the hospital.
- Nathan cannot convince Ira to come with her child. He insists that if he is not too old to build a new life, neither is she. But he can't convince her, so he's grateful when Selvam vows to take care of his sister and nephew.
- Once Nathan and Ruku are dropped off in the city, they realize they are still not sure of exactly where to go. They grow more and more tired and lost, bewildered by the big city.
- They stop to have a snack and a rest, and by the time they have strength enough to again, it's too dark to do anything.
- They go to a temple for food and shelter for the night.
- When the time comes to crowd and bustle for food, Nathan stays on the side.

- He ends up sharing a single portion with Ruku.
- Later, when they realize their bundles have been lost or stolen, Nathan comforts Ruku that at least they still have their money. Nathan tries to make a little joke, and generally seems to accept their misfortune.
- In the morning, Rukmani and Nathan realize they've been robbed.
- They set out again to find Murugan, steeling their hungry bellies. Nathan admits that they are lost, and he can't quite follow any of the directions they've been getting. They rest, and Nathan notes that they might be reduced to begging.
- They watch some street children play for a bit, and Nathan suggests they might ask one of the street children for help.
- They follow Puli, the boy they've gotten to direct them.
- Arriving at the house where Murugan is supposed to be employed, Nathan explains that he's looking for his son.
- Nathan will not be deterred when the servants are unhelpful, and he insists on speaking to the head of the household.
- Nathan is a bit shaken by the fact that the head of the house is a doctor and a woman. He stammers so much that Ruku ends up doing all the talking. The doctor informs the weary travelers that their son, Murugan, now works for the "Collector" and lives at his house. The doctor invites Nathan and Rukmani to stay for dinner at her servant, Das's house.
- After Nathan and Rukmani are invited to dine at Das's house, Nathan is his solid self again. He reminds Rukmani that she'll have to get used to city things, like using the dirty latrine.
- Nathan and Ruku set off to the Collector's House, and both are excited to see their son and new daughter-in-law.
- Finally the two arrive at their son's home. Nathan and Ruku can both sense that they're getting a cool welcome from his wife, Ammu. They are not prepared, however, to learn that Murugan has left her.
- Nathan helpfully suggests that maybe he and his wife could help to look for Murugan, before he's shot down by Murugan's bitter, abandoned wife.
- To diffuse the tension, Nathan emphasizes that he and Ruku will return to their own children in the village
- In another awkward incident as they leave, Nathan confirms to a servant that they won't ever be visiting this place again.
- Rukmani and Nathan settle into temple life and plan how they'll get back to their village.
- When Rukmani comes back to the temple one day with Puli, Nathan is worried that they can't add this extra little burden to their own.
- Still, Nathan warms to Puli when the boy suggests that they can work at the stone quarry for more money.
- Nathan works hard at the quarry alongside Ruku, and as they begin to save up some money, Nathan asks Puli if he might return with them to their village.
- Nathan explains to Puli his need to return home, even if there's nothing there for him.
- One day, leaves the quarry ahead of Ruku and Puli. He returns to the temple telling them he's tired.
- Upon their arrival, with excessive food, Nathan runs off to a corner and vomits. He admits he's been sick all day.
- In spite of his sickness (and the rain that now pours down), Nathan insists on going to work beside Ruku.

- Some time later, Nathan collapses in the mud on a hillside.
- Nathan comes in and out of consciousness on the temple floor where Ruku holds him.
- He says his time has come, and that he would like to go. He is at peace.
- Nathan tells Rukmani not to grieve for him, as he lives on through his children.
- Finally, Nathan reminds Rukmani that they have been happy together.
- Nathan dies at the temple before they are able to return home.

Kenny Character Analysis

Kennington is a white, western doctor (presumably British) who comes in and out of Rukmani's village, helping the people and ultimately building a hospital. Kenny is an interestingly complex character, who is often something of a stereotype symbolizing the difficulty with colonialism. Kenny is committed to helping the people around him, but he views them as different. His aid could be looked at as benevolent charity, but it is also tinged with the fact that Kenny judges the people around him and seems to hold himself to be superior.

Kenny shouldn't be viewed as a villain because he sacrifices himself to help others. Though he is intensely private (another indication that he does not view the Indians as his social peers), Kenny gives up his wife and children, and life, essentially, to be in India. With the coming of the hospital, we see that Kenny lives according to a completely intangible hope. He abstractly believes he can do something to "save" these people, and while it does come from completely good intentions, we've got to question his belief that he's in any position to save anybody.

Kenny does have several saving graces. In the first place, he is incredibly generous with his time and money. For example, he brings food for Rukmani when he can, and treats her, her mother, and Ira. He even gives Nathan and Rukmani ten rupees for their final journey from the village.

More importantly, though, at the end of the novel Kenny's last interaction with Rukmani shows that he's finally starting to understand Indian culture. Kenny started out thinking the people were in need of some philosophical direction and material aid. He judged them as foolish because he didn't fully understand the depth of their poverty and the strength of their spiritual convictions. In Kenny's last talk with Rukmani, he comes to accept that the ways of the West are simply not applicable here. As a result of the difficult circumstances that many Indians face, many people turn to their faith and accept their suffering. When Rukmani mentions that they are in God's hands, we get the sense that Kenny's finally understood that this is the only way people can deal with their situations.

Kenny Timeline and Summary

- Kenny enters the story for the first time when he aids Rukmani's dying mother.
- Kenny and Rukmani's mother seem to have an understanding, and she passes in peace

under his care.
- Kenny notes that there is something sad in Ruku's face, and asks what it is.
- Upon hearing of Ruku's problems with fertility, Kenny says that he can make no promises, but might be able to help a little.
- Kenny notes that Rukmani seems frightened, and he insists that he won't harm her.
- Ultimately Kenny helps Rukmani.
- One day Kenny runs into Rukmani in her field. He chastises her for collecting dung when he runs into her in the fields one day. He points out that the fields need the fertilizer, but he can offer no alternative for what Rukmani's family might use as fuel and sealant in their house.
- Kenny joins Rukmani's family for their midday meal. Though it's clear Kenny is not used to customs like sitting on the floor, he does his best.
- He praises Rukmani and Nathan for their home and children.
- Gradually, Kenny becomes a friend to the family. He brings little gifts and treats for the children, who are particularly fond of him. When Kenny learns that things are getting harder for Ruku's family, he brings what he can, sometimes even milk for the baby.
- Kenny is on the road, where Nathan and Rukmani run into him on their return from their meager rice-buying expedition. Kenny rants and concludes that there is nothing in this country. He curses them for their meekness and wails that there is nothing in this country.
- Kenny is stressed out after long days working at the tannery clinic.
- Still, he pays attention to Rukmani when she finally catches up with him after a long day of work. He chides her for her foolishness when he learns she's still keeping her visits secret from her husband.
- Kenny promises to try to help Rukmani's daughter, Ira, though he stresses he can't guarantee anything.
- Kenny brings news that Murugan is doing well at his new job in the city (a job he got from Kenny's recommendation).
- At one point in the novel, Kenny is a bit taken aback by Rukmani's decision to ask him about his own family. On the other hand, he expresses wonder that they've known each other this long, and this has only come up now.
- Kenny says he has a wife and children at home, but that he isn't bound by them.
- Still, he says he can only handle this country a little at a time, so he must occasionally leave.
- Kenny then closes up, saying he only admitted about his personal background in a moment of lunacy. He firmly makes Ruku promise never to repeat what he's said, and then he slips off.
- The next time Rukmani and Kenny meet in the village, Kenny greets her with his usual strange greeting, not quite friendly, but not hostile.
- Kenny asks after Ruku's family, and then coolly reveals that his wife has left him and his sons have been taught to forget him.
- He adds that Rukmani could never understand his situation. He does responds with some admiration, however, when Rukmani points out that her ways and beliefs are not inferior, just different.
- Kenny then admits that he doesn't really know what country is his home anymore.
- Kenny asks after Ira, and is not surprised that she turned to prostitution; he has seen it happen to other destitute women. Kenny assures Rukmani that once Ira's baby is born, her reputation won't matter.

- He chides her for caring what other people think and notes that this foolish vanity is a problem everywhere in the world.
- Kenny shows Rukmani the plans for the new hospital and explains that he's been collecting funds here in India and abroad as well.
- He reiterates his belief that people need only to cry out for help in order to get it. He becomes irate at Ruku, knowing that she believes suffering is about enduring and spiritual cleansing.
- Instead of trying to reason with her, Kenny admits he'll never understand the people around him and the way they think.
- Kenny still travels to raise funds to build the hospital. He explains to Ruku that he'll make this project work.
- Kenny hires Rukmani's son, Selvam and begins paying him a small wage for his work.
- When Ruku asks Kenny how he'll possibly afford to pay a full staff one day, Kenny insists he'll find the financial means.
- Kenny tends to Nathan and tells Ruku that it's clear the old man worries too much about his family.
- Kenny has no choice but to understand that they're in a difficult position, as Nathan is really the only breadwinner for the family.
- Kenny asks whether any of Ruku's sons could contribute, before it becomes clear to him instantly that he has taken her last hope from her, by taking her son Selvam away from the land. He covers his face with his hands and is clearly pained.
- Kenny asks whether Ruku ever makes significant plans for the future, and he seems to accept the obvious fact that Ruku never does.
- Kenny leaves abruptly after Ruku says they are all in God's hands.

Character Roles

Protagonist

Rukmani

The protagonist is the main character of a novel, and usually one who undergoes some kind of great change. Rukmani goes through many experiences and changes, and in the end she arrives in her home with a completely different life. With no land, no husband, and entirely reliant on her children, she decides to live out her days in quiet reflection. Ruku is not necessarily involved in all of the actions that take place in the book, but she's generally the most prominent of the characters. Events in Ruku's life never occur in a vacuum – she is always with her children or husband, but ultimately she's our protagonist because she's present for all of the actions, and because she embodies the voice of the text.

Antagonist

Nature

Nectar in a Sieve has no single antagonist (traditionally the character who presents an obstacle or major difficulty to the protagonist). This novel is rife with all sorts of difficulties and obstacles, many of them coming from entirely different places. Nature is the primary difficulty for Rukmani

and Nathan, and the uncertainty of nature is an utterly destabilizing factor in Rukmani's life.

Antagonist
The tannery
Rukmani views the tannery as a negative force of change. Like nature, the tannery ushers in good and bad tidings. Though it pollutes the village and takes three of Ruku's sons away from her, it also provides a little income that helps the family get through some of their hardest times. Still, the tannery symbolizes the negative economic changes that Ruku associates with ruining her village and dividing her family. Ultimately the tannery is the great evil that buys Nathan and Ruku's land and takes their home from them. The tannery is not inherently evil but provides obstacles that are destabilizing to Ruku's life and happiness.

Antagonist
Kunthi
Kunthi can also be looked at as an antagonist, as she holds threats over both Nathan and Rukmani. Kunthi extorts the family's final supply of rice during a time of great need by threatening to expose the secrets that husband and wife have kept from each other. Ironically, once the truth comes out between Ruku and Nathan, they're able to forgive and love each other again. We discover that the source of antagonism is not so much Kunthi, as it was the deception between them. Kunthi is antagonistic, but she is also a means of exploiting honestly in any relationship.

Foil
Kenny to Rukmani
Kenny's perspective on life serves as a foil to Rukmani's. He constantly states that people who suffer should cry out for help. Guided by her religious beliefs and her own quiet pride, Rukmani sees the world in a fundamentally different way. People who don't know her have no burden (and likely no inclination) to help her. To her, suffering is a natural and inevitable part of life, and bearing it with dignity is an important part of spiritual purity. Kenny is frustrated by what he sees as acquiescent suffering in the culture around him. While Ruku may suffer in many other ways, she does not suffer from this frustration.

Foil
Kunthi to Rukmani
Kunthi and Rukmani represent opposite sides of femininity. While both are sexual creatures, Ruku confines her sexuality to her husband, while Kunthi has sexual experiences with anyone who possesses willingness and an able pocket. While Ruku guards her sexuality as a sacred expression of love for her husband, Kunthi sees it as an opportunity for physical affirmation and economic progress. Unlike Ruku, Kunthi blames her suffering on other things and people, and naively believes her life will get better once she gets her beauty back. Ruku refused to both place blame and expect charity and bears her suffering with dignity.

Kunthi articulates the difference between her and Ruku early on in the novel: Ruku is a creature of the earth, and proud to be so, while Kunthi views the earth disdainfully, and thinks of herself as fit for greater things. Where Ruku is a modest-looking creature of natural inner beauty and goodness, Kunthi is outwardly beautiful and inwardly ugly, becoming a creature of pitiful and hopeless evil. It's fitting that Kunthi disappears from the story, while Ruku leaves us with a

gentle sense of hopeful endurance.

Character Clues

Family Life

In *Nectar in a Sieve*, the family is the central unite for each individual; every character can be seen for their strengths and weaknesses relative to how they view their position within the family, and to how loyal they are to the family unit. Arjun, Thambi and Murugan desert their family, adding to the general sense of hopelessness, while Selvam and Ira are tied to the family and end up being Ruku's last hope. Nathan and Ruku sacrifice everything they can for their children, and in the end some other characters rise to the occasion to make similar sacrifices, while others don't.

Fertility and one's interactions with children are also central to how the characters function in the novel. We know Ruku most intimately, and she tells us that she sometimes has ungenerous misgivings about children. For example, she weeps to learn Ira is a boy and does not take to Sacrabani immediately. She eventually overcomes her feelings, but she has to think them through, as when she reminds herself that Puli and Sacrabani are just children.

Kenny and Ira in particular show their absolute and unfailing generosity by their interactions with children. Both of them are wonderful with kids in general. Kenny brings treats for Ruku's children (although he has abandoned his only family), and Ira loves Kuti like her own.

Kenny and Ira think of children as the property of the universe. Kunthi, by contrast, has a mean and hard son who is much like her, and in the end, abandons her. It seems that what people give to children mirrors what they receive in return.

Location

The book is divided into something of a pastoral – with the first part in the country and the second in the city. To a certain extent, location determines the kinds of lives that are possible for the characters. As we get to know Ruku in the first part of the book, she's constantly going to the land for spiritual sustenance. In good and bad times, she and Nathan look over the fields and rejoice in the fecundity around them.

By contrast, Kunthi represents the degradation of traditional values. She is proud to call herself someone who has never, and will never, take to the earth. Her dislocation from the soil is symbolic of her moral dislocation. The earth, requiring care and tenderness, is good, and people who are removed from it lack the natural goodness of human morality and kindness.

This idea is magnified when Ruku and Nathan reach the city. The temple people do not rely on their own wits or the land for sustenance, and their humanity has hardened as a result. They do not regard Nathan and Ruku as other people experiencing hard times but simply see them as competitors. Even in her most difficult circumstances in the village, Ruku felt for her neighbors. There is, however, no such community in the city. The people of the city do not share the land, and as such they share no common bond with their fellow man. Children fight over scraps in the

city like animals. This leads Ruku to think of her own children, who suffered from hunger but were raised happily and learned to compassionately share with others.

Ultimately, Markandaya allows the city (and the modernity of urbanization that it represents) to be a symbol of the moral failings and remoteness of humanity. The natural setting of the country is the place in which the good-natured parts of humanity can dwell and grow.

Social Status or Societal Position

Social position is notable in *Nectar in a Sieve* mostly because it is ignored. Rukmani definitely refers to traditional social order, but her own family is the first generation that begins to understand that the old cast rules are being broken down by changing times.

Rukmani's father suffered because the social structure began to favor people like the Collector over the village headman. On the other hand, Ruku's dad contradicted social norms by educating all of his children, girls included. The really important thing to recognize is that Rukmani lives in a time of flux – social order is not so distant as to be unrecognizable, but it is fragile and changing. Ruku's sons first defy convention when they begin to work at the tannery, even though they are of the agricultural caste. Eventually, Ruku comes around to the opinion that making ends meet is more important than following the mandates of their social position.

Ruku disrespects Kunthi for becoming a prostitute (just about the lowest social status), but even Ruku eventually accepts her daughter Ira's prostitution. Again, the family's need makes the traditional social order seem less important. When Ruku meets Ammu, Murugan's abandoned wife, she doesn't even blink at the realization that that Ammu has also taken to selling her body. Ruku's acceptance may signify that the old social order cannot withstand the new needs of modernity.

Finally, Ruku and Nathan discover what it feels like to be looked down upon when they begin to be mistaken for beggars in the city. At first, Ruku obsesses over this and commits herself to buying some things to bring to her daughter-in-law's house so she doesn't look like a beggar. However, as times become difficult, Ruku worries less about appearances. She knows she's not a beggar, and ultimately her tenacity is applied to the practical realities of living, instead of giving way to wounded pride.

Social position is initially important, but it is ultimately not paramount, as traditions change and times get harder. Essentially, social position ends up being exactly the kind of thing that can be dropped as practicality demands.

Literary Devices

Symbols, Imagery, Allegory

Tannery

The tannery is, among many things, a symbol of modernity. It transforms the village

environmentally and economically. It also transforms the relationships between the people within the village. People like Kunthi are glad for the tannery, while Rukmani sees its filthiness and commercialism as a threat to village life. Rukmani loses three sons to the tannery.

As a company, the tannery provided Arjun, Thambi, and Raja each with a different way to deal with their dire poverty. Without this opportunity Ruku's sons might well have turned to the land, rather than turning away from their family. As a symbol of modernity, the tannery allows the boys to think of the larger developments going on in the world. This inspires two of them to leave their own home searching work elsewhere. Just as the tannery represents possibility beyond the family land, it also subtly degrades the importance of family life.

In addition to an economic role, the tannery has a social role in the novel. By working at the tannery, Ruku's sons are breaking caste, or their fixed role within Hindu society. Just as the tannery ignores the tradition of agriculture on the land, it also ignores the tradition's that family's pass down from father to son. With the advent of the tannery, all bets are off. The values of family and tradition are supplanted by the possibilities that come with sprawling industrial modernity.

Water

Nathan and Rukmani name their firstborn child Irawaddy, "after one of the great rivers of Asia, as of all things water was most precious to us." (2.48) There is great emphasis on rice in the novel: when Nathan shows Rukmani the grain of the harvest and promises their prosperity lies in it. Throughout *Nectar in a Sieve*, it becomes increasingly clear that grain and seed are nothing without water. India be hit by the occasional monsoon rains, but rain is nearly impossible to predict on a daily basis.

In some ways, the rain patterns reflect the balance of certainty and uncertainty that characterize Rukmani's view of the world: good times and bad times will both come, but how intense, and when, can never be predicted. It is best to accept the uncertainty and do what one can with what one has, just as one either waits for the rain or wishes it to end.

The first troubles of the family come just after Ira's wedding, when a heavy and incessant downpour drowns the rice fields and ensures that there won't be much eating that year (7.4). The next great catastrophe is a terrible drought (13.1). The marks the first time Nathan and Ruku are threatened with the loss of their land. The two have to sell nearly everything they own just to keep the land, and of course after all of their most prized possessions are gone, the rain comes again.

The effect of the drought, and the starvation that looms bring some of the family's saddest times. First, Rukmani and Nathan discover the fissures in their marriages (Ruku's infertility treatment, Nathan's infidelity) when Kunthi uses their secrets against them to rob them of their last food rations. Secondly, because the family must scrounge for scraps and garbage to eat, Ira turns to prostitution. Finally, the youngest son, Kuti, dies. Ultimately, all of this could have been avoided had the rains come earlier, leading the crops to come out sooner.

The impact of water on the crops and harvests is evident enough, but water seems to show up as an important symbol in times of scarcity and plenty. During the drought, the tannery has a

reservoir that the people of the village to rely on (13.72). The implication here seems to be that when nature doesn't provide, industry can. This gets to the heart of the mixed feelings surrounding the tannery.

Water is also an important element of Nathan's death: it drizzles the day he becomes ill, and by the time he dies, there's an unrelenting downpour. Even the reliable light that usually burns atop the temple has been dampened out by the water, prompting Rukmani to maddeningly repeat, "Fire cannot burn in water!" (29.2). When Rukmani cries out in futility against the water, it's as if she's admitting that no amount of hope (fire) can stand up in the face of nature's great inevitability, death. The rain has increased as Nathan's strength has dwindled. The water is linked to Nathan's impending doom as proof that whatever will be, will be.

Water is also important as a symbol for the women. In the most obvious case, consider that Ira is named for a river. In addition, like the women of *Nectar in a Sieve*, water gives life and takes it away. Rukmani bears many children (giving life), but Kunthi, for instance, has the power to destroy Nathan and Rukmani's lives by blackmailing them and stealing their food in a time of starvation.

Water is a good thing in moderation, but too much or too little can be deadly. The same reasoning can apply to women's sexuality in this novel. When a woman's body is dry (or infertile) it can mean her downfall, while prostitution in the case of Ira and Kunthi is a prime example of a woman's body being too ripe. In this novel, women's sexuality, like water, must be in moderation, or dangerous consequences could follow.

Learning

Learning is another symbol of hope in *Nectar in a Sieve*. As is the case for so much in the novel, education is a double-edged sword. Ruku's father decided to educate his children, even the girls, which was unusual in that setting. Ruku's father had once been an important man, and people of her village once said he taught his children because he wanted them to be a cut above the rest, but Ruku states she thinks her father knew that learning would be a comfort to them in whatever times of misery they might later face (2.14). No matter what hardships occur, learning can never be taken away.

Nathan's reaction to Rukmani's education is also an important opportunity for him to prove he is an unusual husband. When Ruku is pregnant with Ira, she takes to writing again. Nathan is illiterate, and when he sees Ruku writing, he might well resent it as a marker of his own inadequacy compared to his wife. Instead, he sees it as another reason to be proud of her. This acceptance demonstrates that he is secure and loves her in spite of what tradition might dictate is the appropriate role for a woman (2.21).

Ruku teaches her own children how to read and write, and they eventually surpass her in ability. Her teaching allows her boys, Arjun and Thambi, to become the spokesmen for the strike at the tannery. While neighbors in the village may think that their learning is to blame (22.1), one might actually think that learning was blameless in the process – it just gave the boys the medium, confidence, and ability to express the frustrations they would have had anyway.

In Ruku's hardest times, when she and Nathan realize they are homeless and penniless in a

foreign city, Ruku turns again to learning. She thinks her literacy might bring in some money, so she decides to be a letter writer at market. While she bears some of the scorn of the city-people, who are unaccustomed to seeing a literate woman, the confidence she exudes is all she needs to earn the few annas that will help her and Nathan live (27.12).

Finally, Selvam's learning ends up being most central to the plot. He had never really taken to the land, and his education allowed him other opportunities. He becomes a quick study of Kenny's, and ultimately it is his ability that will support the whole family once Ruku and Puli return to the village. Selvam's learning, though it may have seemed unnecessary for agricultural farming, ends up being his saving grace.

Drums

Drums in *Nectar in a Sieve* symbolize times of great change. Our introduction to drumming occurs at Ira's wedding (6.11): a drummer joins with a fiddler to make up a whole band. Then, as the miserable storm that drowns the fields and nearly destroys the town subsides, Ruku listens to the incessant "drums of calamity" beating for the whole town to hear (7.25). In their rhythm, she says she hears "the impotence of human endeavor." Worse, the silences are more ominous than the beats themselves, as they seem to only signal greater and incessant doom. Just as a silence following a beat will always be followed by another beat, Ruku is sure her disasters will pile one upon the other.

The next instance of drumming occurs at Deepavali, the Festival of Lights (10.8). It is an upbeat time in Ruku and Nathan's lives, as food is no longer scarce. Their fortunes have shifted away from hunger, and the drumming of that night signals a change in rhythm, which will lead to the conception of their last baby, Kuti. These drums brought a child to Ruku, but the next ones will take boys from her. Workers show up in the town beating drums, calling men to come to Ceylon (12.34). Arjun and Thambi, who have just left the tannery, decide that their lives must march on (with our without their family), so they follow the call to a far-off land.

Drums take on another meaning when they are present at Raja's death (15.8). The drums begin on the morning Raja is to be cremated. As is customary, the women stay behind instead of attending the actual cremation. Ruku listens to the drum-beats, and when they finally stop, it is a signal to Ruku that the burning is complete, and that Raja's body is no more. The drums here seem to symbolize life as a drum beat, a reliable thing that ticks on so long as the heart has beats left in it.

The dum-dum carts that Ruku buy for Puli and Sacrabani represent the final instance of drum-like rhythms in the book. Puli's little beat following them along as he pulls the cart behind him symbolizes Ruku's endurance against all odds. The little toys are with her when she and Puli return to the village. It's notable that Puli clutches the silent cart in his arms in his moment of hesitation over being welcomed to Puli's family. But Ira's immediate warm acceptance of him is a hint to the reader that he will soon joyously pull the cart, with its little drumbeat, behind him again.

Setting

Rural India, a city in India

Place

Part One of the novel takes place in an unnamed village in rural India, while Part Two takes place in an unnamed major city in urban India. Markandaya's decision to avoid specifics is deliberate: the fact is that the first part of the story could take place in any part of any agricultural nation, and the second part in among any sector of the urban poor. This lack of specificity opens the scope of *Nectar in a Sieve*: this story could apply to families other than Rukmani's. The important thing is that our characters go from subsistence living in a largely agricultural economy, to barely making a living in a city economy.

Times are changing, and industrialization is encroaching on the rural areas, so the agriculture and working classes are forced to move into similar situations of poverty in urban landscapes. This could be just as easily be a story in today's world: imagine a Montana man's family's corn farm being bought out by big agri-business, forcing him to move to an unfamiliar factory job in a city. The plight of modernity is universal, and while the details are rooted in India, the story belongs to anyone who's ever moved from country to town as a result of poverty.

This element of moving also makes the story something of a pastoral: one of those tropes where the country life is represented as sometimes idyllic and generally better than city life. In this novel, the beauty of the landscape is almost a reflection of the goodness of the people on the land. Though bad things do happen in Ruku's village, people in the city seem infinitely worse-off. Only in the city does Ruku see people push the crippled and scrounge for food like animals. The implication is that people are most natural in rural surroundings. When they are taken out of these surroundings and thrust into the dirty artificiality of the city, they lose a bit of their.

It's notable that the novel's most evil character, Kunthi, proudly argues that she's not tied to the earth, whereas morally upstanding Ruku celebrates and reveres the earth. In this pastoral reading, the goodness of the earth is a moral reflection of the goodness of people, and a polluted earth (i.e. the city) is a stronghold for the morally weak, thieves, crooks, and generally antagonistic people.

Time

Markandaya avoids a specific timeframe in the novel, which makes the notion of time ambiguous. There is, however, a lot to interpret in the ambiguity. One argument can be made is that that the book anticipates India's colonial independence (so it's before 1947). On the other hand, some say that Markandaya's fictitious world may be a reflection on the country *after* India's independence.

India was a colony of Britain from 1858 until 1947, but the movement had begun much earlier. Markandaya's novel was published in 1954 but it was most likely written earlier, when Indian independence was a controversial topic. Most critics locate the work relative to that important year of 1947: the year of Indian independence and the partition of India into India and Pakistan.

Though Markandaya avoids dates, we get some details that are helpful in locating the book within the broader history of India.

However, you could argue that the events of the novel take place post-independence. The fact that Muslims are regarded as foreign, and that the economy is moving from being solely agricultural to more in line with international industrial practices hint that this might be a post-colonial India. (For more on this, see the Historical Shout-Outs section.)

Still, there's a case to be made that Ruku's India is about the time *before* Independence. Ruku's attitude towards life is that external circumstances are what they are, and that there's no reason to fight them. Her attitude towards her sons' agitation at the tannery for higher wages demonstrates that she often favors passivity in the face of stronger forces. This kind of attitude is exactly contrary to the teachings of India's great liberation leader, Gandhi. Gandhi encouraged Indians to realize that they could fight for a better life, rather than continuing to accept the status quo of being inferior to the British.

Unlike Ruku, Gandhi talked of rights and justice; her language is more aligned with the pre-Gandhi way of thinking. However, Rukmani's sons seem to reflect Gandhi's teachings. Even if they don't speak specifically of Gandhi, and even if they seem to pre-date Gandhi, this younger generation represented by Ruku's sons embodies the changing attitude in India. This might mean that independence, and the ideology that came with it, were still on the horizon.

Further evidence that the book dates from pre-independence India might be found in the influence of white people in India. Ruku explicitly says that Kenny has power as a white man. Such an acknowledgment would not be an appropriate belief during a time when India had just forced the white British Empire out of its affairs. Kenny's entire hospital endeavor is also exemplary of the kind of projects the British set up in their colonial campaign to "civilize" the Indian natives. Kenny might be a modern Peace Corps volunteer, spreading the benefits of modernity to the rest of the world.

This novel's relationship to a specific time in India's political history is unclear; there is certainly more than one time period in which the work can be situated. The take-home message, though, is that Markandaya explicitly avoids having this political conversation, and in some ways, tries to elevate the book beyond political details. Without anchors in a specific time or place, the novel is allowed to be a more universal story about a family trying to make it against great odds. Without the burden of politics and history, we can focus on the emotional and dramatic import of the story.

Narrator Point of View

Narrative Voice: First Person (Central Narrator)
Rukmani is the narrator of her own story, which she tells in a flashback. As with any story told in the first person, it's important to remember that everything the narrator tells is selected for a reason. Thus every detail she includes (like the phrase she repeats to herself as Nathan is

dying) and every detail she deliberately *excludes* (like what exactly Kenny did for her infertility) is deliberate. What Ruku chooses to tell us ends up being a reflection of Ruku's own values and personality. The events of the story take on an added meaning when we realize they're excerpts of an entire life. What Rukmani shares with us are those special moments that a dying woman reflecting on her life thinks are important.

This flashback point of view allows the whole story to be Ruku's own *reflections* on her own life. She tells us the story as past tense, and she occasionally adds foreshadowing and interpretation that she couldn't have known at the time. These little "notes from the future" are "present Ruku" interpreting "past Ruku." When they happen, they're important markers. In regular first-person mode, a narrator is able to tell a compelling and straightforward story. The usage of first-person flashbacks, though, is an opportunity to elevate the simple narrative to thoughtful reflection without cluttering the story itself.

Genre

Literary Fiction, Semi-Autobiographical

Literary Fiction

Markandaya's novel is a literary account of a changing India. Still, it doesn't focus on political or economic details, instead choosing to follow only one matriarch. Markandaya's narrative is successful in eschewing specifics while still presenting symbols, events, and characters that tell us about the onslaught of modernity in India. Though the book can rightly be read as a story of India's transition into the post-colonial era, it is important that many of these details are left out. This is a deftly crafted personal narrative that can be understood as a universal tale of family, hope, and endurance. The specific details (in some readings) can melt into the background, as there's enough richness in the psychological complexity of the characters and the meaning of the events to supplant a purely political reading.

Semi-Autobiographical

Some people might argue that the book is semi-autobiographical, as Markandaya was an Indian woman living around the time of Rukmani. Actually, Markandaya was the daughter of a rail transport officer, and she attended the University of Madras for writing and freelance journalism. Though she didn't finish her degree, she did move to England, where she married an Englishman, did some secretarial work and other jobs she described as "dull but amiable," and went on to become a canonical Indian woman Commonwealth writer. That's definitely a far cry from Ruku's life.

Still, though Markandaya's life wasn't all that similar to Ruku's. Markandaya was incredibly sympathetic to the causes of the rural poor in India, and likely saw much poverty while traveling South India with her father by rail. She was also influenced by Gandhi's efforts to highlight the plight of rural Indians in poverty under British rule.

Tone

Non-judgmental, Thoughtful

Markandaya is an Indian writer living in England and writing in English about a life of rural poverty that is not exactly her own. Markandaya was sometimes criticized as less than authentic because she didn't live the rural poverty-stricken existence about which she writes. She often countered that her physical distance from India gave her the power to objectively comment on what she observed.

This defense certainly resonates when we think about Markandaya's portrayal of her characters' actions and thoughts. She addresses the best and worst aspects of rural life and poverty (which she saw firsthand traveling through South India), but she doesn't get caught up in romanticizing (or vilifying) aspects of daily village life. Instead, she imbues her characters, particularly Rukmani, with strengths and weaknesses that essentially typify the rural Indian existence. Rukmani is hopeful and enduring, but she often reacts with emotion when it comes to her family. Markandaya sympathizes with her characters, but she manages to ground their emotion in very real events.

Because Markandaya has a sense of the reality of living in rural India, her characters are realistic. Most importantly, our narrator Rukmani embodies Markandaya's reflective attitude. The author's objective eye is given voice in the narrator's realistic reflections. For instance, Markandaya may know that there is an inherent controversy in having a foreign doctor battle the problems of infertility. Rukmani's own interactions with Kenny, sometimes edgy, sometimes shy, capture that tension without any high-handed declarations about the significance and implications of colonialism.

Ultimately, Markandaya's distance to her own Indian culture serves as both a strength and weakness to her writing.

Writing Style

Simple, Subtle, Honest, Earnest

Rukmani's narrative is presented in a matter-of-fact style. She doesn't abstract or intellectualize her circumstances. Often she gives the reader a "this happened, then this, then this" account.

However, what makes the text interesting are the occasional dreamlike pauses or asides from the narrative that give us a peek into Rukmani's actual feelings. When Rukmani talks of her wedding night, she does it with reference to the many examples of romantic nights that she and Nathan shared. This is a subtle hint that her arranged marriage has produced genuine love.

We get a similar window into Rukmani's thoughts when she buys the cart for Puli. Initially she resists making the expensive purchase, but she relents when she remembers that no matter

what else, Puli is still a child. She then buys a cart for her grandson Sacrabani. Though she's described Sacrabani as a strange child, this gesture clues in the reader on the idea that Ruku has come to similar conclusions about Puli and Sacrabani. Without a specific word about her decision, Rukmani communicates that she had has some insensitive feelings, but that she's gotten over them by thinking more broadly.

Rukmani is open about her failings – her petty and selfish thoughts are as available to us as her lofty and noble ones. For example, Ruku admits that when Selvam is quiet as he hears about the land being sold, she immediately thinks he is selfish and doesn't care about the family's situation. This thought is pretty harsh, especially after Selvam has been so good to the family. Ruku puts it out there, and then deals with it immediately, chiding herself for having thought it. Also, she says she can't help Janaki when Janaki's family is forced to leave town, and she admits that she can't afford to think about where they'll go. We excuse these seemingly mean-spirited thoughts, when Ruku thinks fondly of Janaki again during the joyous celebration of Deepavali.

Ruku is honest with us about her limitations. We see through her sincere and open prose that she is a good woman, who is trying hard to be a better person. For her honesty, we trust her. The private details, misgivings, failings, and joys that she shares openly only inspire us to believe that she's earnest of feeling and spirit.

What's Up With the Title?

The line "Nectar in a Sieve" is taken from a poem by Samuel Taylor Coleridge, which you can read about in "What's Up with the Epigraph." Without analyzing the poem, the title alone reflects something of the book: nectar is a lovely liquid that will eventually drain away when put into a sieve (a sifter). The title is a beautiful way to talk about the inevitable draining of life in the face of suffering and death. The events of the novel parallel this theme quite closely. The title cast the beauty and the misery of life next to each other, and raises the question of which has the upper hand, the nectar of life, or the sieve of destruction.

What's Up With the Epigraph?

"Work without hope draws nectar in a sieve, And hope without an object cannot live."

The epigraph comes from the 1825 poem "Work without Hope" by the English Romantic poet, Samuel Taylor Coleridge.

ALL Nature seems at work. Slugs leave their lair—
The bees are stirring—birds are on the wing—
And Winter, slumbering in the open air,
Wears on his smiling face a dream of Spring!
And I, the while, the sole unbusy thing,
Nor honey make, nor pair, nor build, nor sing.

Yet well I ken the banks where amaranths blow,

Have traced the fount whence streams of nectar flow.
Bloom, O ye amaranths! bloom for whom ye may,
For me ye bloom not! Glide, rich streams, away!
With lips unbrighten'd, wreathless brow, I stroll:
And would you learn the spells that drowse my soul?
Work without Hope draws nectar in a sieve,
And Hope without an object cannot live.

The poem is an unconventional sonnet; it develops a main idea in the first twelve lines, and is capped by a big thought in the final couplet. The poem follows a narrator describing the industriousness of nature's creatures, preparing for the coming spring. All of Creation is at work, but the speaker is sullen as the only creature he can see who finds himself without an occupation.

He notes that while he is a part of Nature, the world does not work for him. For example, it is not for him that the amaranths (flowers) bloom, and he watches as the richness of Nature escapes from him in the streams. In the final couplet the speaker sums up his despair and explains the ultimate reason for his listlessness: he cannot work as he has no hope. He has nothing to hope for, and so he has no life to speak of. He is an observer, not a participant, in the wealth of the natural world, and as he does not partake in it, he does not receive its bounty.

Markandaya uses this poem's final couplet as an epigraph to hint that the problem described in the poem will be a central issue in the novel. Our characters here are awed by the beauty and richness of nature, but they do not always receive happiness from it. Their work is never-ending. Unlike the poem's speaker, however, the characters in *Nectar in a Sieve* are constantly at work, but their work only provides enough to survive and not to celebrate. We learn throughout the novel that survival itself is never a certainty.

Markandaya's use of the poem in *Nectar in a Sieve* is ambiguous. The epigraph puts forth, but does not answer, the question of whether the characters actually have hope. The preceding parts of the poem – which Markandaya deliberately leaves out – make it clear that Coleridge's speaker is hopeless. Markandaya, however, gives no such certainty about her characters. Ruku, Nathan, and the others might have an object for their hope, and their work might not be in vain. If they work in vain, then their doom is certain; if they work towards survival or spiritual redemption, then their efforts become meaningful.

Thus the epigraph captures the central tension of the book: the beginning and end of the book never explicitly tell us whether Rukmani and her family suffer in vain. The characters of the book identify with the idea that work without hope is like nectar draining from a sieve. It is up to the reader, though, to decide whether these characters are actually working without hope. If the characters are buoyed by their hope and work, they may get to enjoy the nectar of life before it slips away.

What's Up With the Ending?

The ending of the book can be seen as an open-ended passageway asking the reader to imagine the rest of Ruku's life. Within the context of the narrative structure, the ending marks the completion point in the circle of Ruku's story. Ruku literally begins chapter one by telling her story in hindsight. The present captures the final days of Rukmani's life as she reminisces on what has come before. As narrator, Rukmani takes us on a tour through the past events that lead up to the present.

The ending of the novel is satisfying as a closure to one chapter of Ruku's life, but the beginning of the novel marks the close to Ruku's real life story. At the beginning of *Nectar in a Sieve* we see that she is with her children and grandchildren, and that her adopted son, Puli, is still with her, having staved off fatal leprosy. Ruku has lost her husband and is losing her sight, and her life is coming to a close.

It's important that the book opens, but doesn't end, with Ruku's consideration of her dying days. If Ruku faced death at the structural end of the novel, the whole affair would be a clear story about the fruitlessness of suffering, a tale of misery capped by death. Instead, Ruku ends the novel on a hopeful note. She has returned home to her happy place, has her family by her side, and a new chapter of her life lies before her. We know she is aging, and so her dying days are inevitably upon her, but Markandaya doesn't want her death to be the take-home message of the whole novel.

Instead, as scholar Indira Ganeshan notes in her introduction to the novel, the book ends with the word "later," which can be taken to indicate promise and hope of the future. The end of the book invites the reader to imagine the future. To learn what actually happens "later," one need only to flip to page one. But to feel the inspiring promise and endurance of the future-which is the real gift of Markandaya's novel-one needs only to close the book, and rest thoughtfully on its final word.

Did You Know?

Trivia

- Kamala Markandaya's personal life is somewhat of a mystery. A World Author Series biography of her stalled for a long time, as no one could pin down obvious personal details. One writer likened her to an Indian temple sculptor who leaves behind artistic masterpieces but not a word about herself. (Source)

Steaminess Rating

PG

There's only one sex scene in *Nectar in a Sieve*, and outside of that one discussion there's not much in the way of explicit sexual description. Instead, sexuality is more present in the book as a dangerous force.

There's a dichotomy between sex within love and sex outside of it. Rukmani remembers being nervous on her wedding night, but she pretty openly says she gets better at sex as her relationship and body mature. (Remember, she's twelve when she gets married.) Nathan and Ruku's night of passion during Deepavali is beautiful and lush, but represent the exception and not the rule. Sex is more often discussed as one of the dark sides of necessity in the context of poverty and the rise of prostitution.

Kunthi and Ira turn to prostitution. Both women gain some power in exchange for sex. Ira gets to feed the ailing Kuti, while Kunthi gets some affirmation of her beauty from the attention she receives from men, and eventually their payment is what begins to sustain her financially.

Women's sexuality gives them power, including the power to make money through prostitution. In a society where women don't have many options, sex may be one of the few ways in which they can assert themselves as breadwinners. This brand of sexuality is threatening to other women (like Ruku) but its most interesting effect is on men. On the one hand men want women for their sexuality, but their excessive sexuality precludes women from being objects of love and respect. In a world where economic necessity can trump the finer points of life, some women have no where to turn but selling themselves.

Allusions and Cultural References

Literature and Philosophy
Samuel Coleridge (epigraph)

Best of the Web

Movie or TV Productions
Pather Panchali
http://www.imdb.com/title/tt0048473/
Nectar in a Sieve has not had a film version, but if you're looking for a similar story, check out *Pather Panchali*, by acclaimed director Satyajit Ray. It's Ray's directorial debut, about a family living in poverty in an unnamed time in an unnamed part of rural India. (Sounds familiar, huh?) Domestic loyalty, agriculture, the beauty of the land, and writing are significant parts of this film,

making it an interesting parallel to *Nectar in a Sieve*.

Images
The Author
http://www.lifeinlegacy.com/2004/0605/MarkandayaKamala.jpg
A young Kamala Markandaya

The Author
http://www.sawnet.org/books/images/kamala_m.jpg
An older Kamala Markandaya

Documents
Perspectives on Indian Fiction in English
http://books.google.com/books?hl=en&lr=&id=MW1rYykQvZ0C&oi=fnd&pg=PA161&dq=%22Nectar+in+a+Sieve%22&ots=XoY1q9QjLv&sig=BAJDCwMyI1fZEJH5hjGdPJs0TPg#PPA166,M1
Excerpts from the chapter on Kamala Markandaya of M. K. Naik's critical study, called *Perspectives on Indian Fiction in English*.

Author Obituary
http://query.nytimes.com/gst/fullpage.html?res=9C02E4DE103EF93BA15756C0A9629C8B63&scp=1&sq=%22Nectar+in+a+Sieve%22&st=nyt
The *New York Times* Obituary of Kamala Markandaya, with an interesting note on her relevance in changing Indian literature.

"Work Without Hope"
http://www.orgs.muohio.edu/anthologies/bijou/vissat/Workwithouthope.htm
An interesting, albeit brief, analysis of Coleridge's poem used for the title and epigraph.

Websites
Author Biography
http://www.beilharz.com/autores/markandaya/
Some background on Kamala Markandaya, as reflected upon at her death.

Made in the USA
Lexington, KY
15 February 2011